10-15-64

A TREASURE TO SHARE

Once there was an apprentice cobbler who was pastor of a Baptist church in England. He could not forget the vision he had of preaching the gospel to the non-Christians of the world, and in a sermon preached in 1792 he cried:

  "Expect great things from God; attempt great things for God!"

Said his friends, then, to William Carey:
"Do you go down — and we will hold the rope."

To the rope-holders of Kuji this book is gratefully dedicated.

A TREASURE

TO SHARE

Elizabeth Anne Hemphill

THE JUDSON PRESS, *Valley Forge*

A TREASURE TO SHARE
Copyright © 1964
THE JUDSON PRESS
Valley Forge, Pa.

Library of Congress Catalog Card No. 64-20501

Printed in the United States of America

FOREWORD

Now it must be told! It is the story of a pioneer missionary in Northern Japan. Like all trail blazers, Miss Thomasine Allen (known far and wide as "Tommy") has followed a vision leading her through unbelievable struggle filled with tears and heartbreak. Not only has she served as an American Baptist missionary in her beloved Japan for over forty years, but she has opened up a great new mission field.

She went out to Japan as a teacher in one of our denominational schools, but the underprivileged children in Iwate Ken on the coast and in the mountain areas of the north called to her. With straw mats under the trees she began Vacation Bible Schools — and then the dream for a kindergarten and mission began to take form. Always the needs of a growing, challenging work have been far greater than the resources.

Her story is one of joy and pathos, laughter and tears. Throughout it all the winsome personality and deep faith of Thomasine Allen shine forth. God has used a life to bring thousands of children and young people to know him and to find abundant life. Kuji, at the end of the railroad, and Tommy are synonymous.

Blanche Moore Hodge

PREFACE

No ONE WRITES A BOOK ALL ALONE. A really inclusive list of all of those who helped in the writing of this book would be a little longer than the text itself. I cannot thank by name the many friends in the United States and in Japan, representing not only all branches of Christianity, but several non-Christian faiths, as well, who took the time to answer questions and guide me to reference material, and offered generous hospitality during my trips to Japan in 1959 and 1961. To all of these friends I am deeply grateful.

But there are a few to whom one must say, "Without your help, this book could not have been written."

My husband, Robert F. Hemphill, encouraged me to make two trips to Japan for research, and patiently lived in an occasionally disorganized household as the book was written. He was always willing to read proof, to help with the research, and to bring his knowledge of the English language to bear on the problems of tense and syntax in which I was occasionally ensnarled.

My friend and neighbor, Joyce Thomann, not only typed the book manuscript and a thesis on the Kuji Center, but she also insisted that she had enjoyed doing it.

Mr. Cyril Bryant, of the Baptist World Alliance, offered invaluable reference material, abiding interest, and unfailing encouragement.

The late Dr. Paul S. Mayer, veteran missionary of the Evangelical United Brethren Church, answered questions, provided insights, and made available his own private library for research.

The late Dr. Clifton E. Olmstead, Professor of Religion at the George Washington University, gave me an understanding of the development of church history. The high standards which he set and his patient and courteous guidance were an inspiration to all of his students.

To these, and to the many other friends who have a share in this book, I offer my profound gratitude.

ELIZABETH ANNE HEMPHILL

CONTENTS

Chapter One

A PLACE WHERE NOTHING WAS KNOWN

IT IS AN HOUR BEFORE MIDNIGHT when the train departs Tokyo's Ueno Station bound for the north. Taxis crowd together and completely jam the four lanes in front of the station, leaving latecomers to thread their way through the nearby labyrinth of streets until they can dart into openings at the station entrance. Here are gathered a group of workmen carrying signs and red banners; they are coal miners who have come to the city to protest the provisions in their new contracts. Just inside the station another group clad in heavy clothing and stout shoes is gathering, and they carry skis and poles and ice skates. They are bound for the magnificent mountain slopes that attract winter sportsmen from all over Japan. In between the coal miners and the skiers throngs of travelers rush intently through the main entrance and spread out along the train tracks to board the cars which will leave on split-second schedules. *Akabos*, porters in dark blue uniforms and red caps, carry piles of luggage from the station entrance to the trains. They strap the suitcases together and race off to the cars, leaving panting travelers well in the rear.

This is the start of a journey to Kuji. The eleven o'clock train leaves the Ueno Station exactly on time, and by midnight the passengers have settled down for the night. In the third-class sleepers they make themselves as comfortable as possible in wooden berths, but in the luxurious second- and first-class cars the more affluent travelers stretch out in reclining chairs or in spotless, comfortable berths. A clean, starched cotton kimono is provided in each berth, as is done in Japanese inns.

11

And so the train steams northward through the night. Leaving behind the industrial suburbs of Tokyo, it crosses the bountiful rice fields of the Kanto plain and passes through the city of Sendai. The pine islands which surround Sendai slip behind the train unnoticed by its sleeping passengers, but by the time the train reaches its next metropolitan stop, many of the travelers are awake and hungry for breakfast. During the extended stop in Morioka they pour from the train to buy tiny earthenware pots of tea, box lunches of rice balls and fish, or ice cream, fruit, and soft drinks. Experienced travelers buy boxes of broiled eel on rice, a particular delicacy of the region.

At nine o'clock in the morning the train leaves Morioka and continues northward toward the port city of Aomori. The railway tracks follow an ancient military road which in feudal times connected the provincial northern cities with Tokyo. Now the train is leaving behind more than a city and more than a provincial capital; modern Japan itself is slipping into the distance as the train moves into northeastern Japan. Surrounding the train are rural villages that are physically a part of modern Japan but which, in many ways, linger in the nineteenth century.

The Kuji-bound traveler must leave the train at the Shiriuchi junction. Here he climbs a flight of stairs, crosses the tracks on an overpass, and descends to the Shiriuchi Station. There is a wait of two hours before the local train to Kuji departs. The traveler may stroll through the town or refresh himself with tea, soft drinks, or *soba,* a dish of Chinese noodles in broth spiced with red pepper and sprinkled with chopped onion.

The train to Kuji is not the luxurious express which has deposited the Kuji-bound traveler in the little town of Shiriuchi. A narrow-gauge local line connects the coastal city of Kuji with the main rail line, and on the two daily runs it carries a variety of goods and passengers. Good-natured country people stream on board carrying boxes and bundles of huge dimension and diversified contents. Vegetable peddlers lug bundles of eggplant, leeks, and giant white radishes, while fish peddlers lift a more odorous cargo aboard the train. With every seat taken and the aisles jammed with passengers and their gear, the little train pulls out of Shiriuchi and winds its way along the coast to reach Kuji two and a half hours later. Lunches are unwrapped and shared, cigarettes are lighted, and playing cards are brought out. The train to Kuji is more than transportation — news and gossip are bartered along with fish and vegetables. Kuji is the end of the line, and here the remaining travelers shoulder their loads, collect their children, and leave the train. Then the trainmen begin to sweep the orange peelings, lunch boxes, and pop bottles down the aisle toward the open door.

At first glance Kuji is just one more rural city. Surrounded by mountains and rice paddies, it lives a life apart from the booming industry and rushing cities of modern Japan. Here country houses of unpainted wood, weathered a soft silvery-grey, dot the roads. Some have thatched roofs tinged with green in summer time, and occasionally scarlet flowers grow along the eaves. Shops wind along the main streets of Kuji with hardware stores displaying bright gold metal pans, dry goods stores showing bolts of material — blue and white cotton in the summer months and deeper and richer colors in the winter time — and small food stores selling fish, vegetables, fruits, and rice. In a tiny kitchen one family bakes fresh rice crackers dotted with sesame seeds, and farther along the street a friendly, buxom woman skewers small fish on bamboo and broils them over charcoal. There are public buildings such as the post office and the city hall, and the movie theatre is marked by gaudy posters advertising the current film.

But Kuji is not just one more rural city. Kuji is the site of a remarkable Christian Center which is slowly but effectively demonstrating to the country people that Christianity is meaningful to the workers in fields, rice paddies, and small shops, as well as to the middle-class parishioners in city churches. Kuji Christian Center, through its work in kindergarten, school, hospital, and farm, is known to hundreds of Japanese in the town itself and in the surrounding villages. This Center was started in 1938 by Miss Thomasine Allen, a missionary of the Woman's American Baptist Foreign Mission Society, as an experiment in Christian living. The farmers, fishermen, policemen, teachers, and shopkeepers who are members of the First Baptist Church of Kuji believe that Christianity is a way of life, not just another religion; and they believe that it is relevant to their lives and to those of their neighbors.

One hot summer day in 1962 a group of young Japanese farmers knocked at the door of Miss Allen's home at the Center. As she opened the door, the leader of the group bowed and introduced his friends. He explained that he knew something of the work of the Center because he had attended a week-long gospel school held for farmers, and now he had brought his family and some of his neighbors to see the Center. They had visited the school and hospital, and they had looked in at the library; now he wondered if they could see Miss Allen's western-style house, and would she please speak to them for a few minutes on faith? Twenty black heads bobbed as the group filed into the hall and slipped off their shoes. After a tour of the house the group assembled in Miss Allen's living room for cookies and tea and for a little talk on faith.

Now in her seventies Miss Allen is tall and vigorous, and only her grey hair suggests the years that have slipped by during her service in Japan. Her face, seldom caught in repose, mirrors the mixture of spiritual depth and outrageous humor that charms both Japanese and Americans. Now, dressed in a fresh cotton print dress, she settled herself in her chair, leaned forward, and began to speak to her guests.

 Many people, both American and Japanese, ask me why on earth I ever came to an isolated place like Kuji. And I tell them the reason: I have a very great treasure that I want to share.

When I came here in 1938, there was no Christian work in this county at all. The people knew nothing about Christianity, and many of them had not even heard the name of Jesus. Instead of staying in the city, where there were many churches, kindergartens, and Christian workers, I thought it would be better to go to a place where *nothing was known.* From a survey I learned that no Christian work was being done in this entire area, and so for that reason I came to Kuji.

It was my thought to begin with the children. First, we opened a kindergarten to instill some of the fundamental teachings into the hearts of boys and girls, and then we opened a primary school so that we could have them a little longer and give them character training.

And then, because the heart and soul cannot be separated

from the body, we opened a hospital so that God could work through the body as well as the soul. God wanted whole bodies and whole souls, and we tried to treat the body, too.

With the farm and the dairy farm school we hope to help raise the standard of living among the farmers by acquainting them with a new diet and a new way of physical living. But with these we must help them know the love of God as well as a love for man, and a love for the soil. Without a Christian background and Christian training it will be hard to raise the farmer's level; the two must go together — body and heart.

In each form of work we have, our aim is to create character — Christian character. We try to put our words into practice.

The sun-flooded room was quiet; a boy in clean, white overalls nodded his head thoughtfully while the man next to him looked wary, skeptical, and questioning. As assent and dissent rippled through the room, Miss Allen continued.

 What is the happy life? It comes from the heart. We should love one another; we should be kind; we should always be thankful. But the world's teaching is entirely different. Blessed are the rich, blessed are those who can play and do not have to work and support themselves. Yet, that doesn't make you happy; real happiness comes from an inner experience.

With deep bows and a flow of courteous Japanese expressions of gratitude, the young farmers prepared to take their leave. The mother of the two small boys adjusted the carrying strap which held the baby on her back, and the other brother, prompted by his watchful father, bowed low. They slipped on their shoes in the entryway and stepped out into the bright sunshine to return to their homes.

In 1958 nearly everyone in Kuji celebrated the Fourth of July. Red and white bunting signaled to all that this was a special occasion. All of the Center buildings were shining clean, and beautiful flower arrangements added to their freshness. Inside the kindergarten auditorium distinguished guests and speakers gathered on the platform before a rapt and respectful audience: The Governor of Iwate Prefecture and his lady, the Mayor of

 Wherever the lantern appears opposite a quotation in this book, it is a reminder that these are the actual words of Thomasine Allen, usually as tape recorded in conversations with the author.

Kuji, Bishop Tomojiro Obara of the Holiness Church, an emissary
from Dr. Toyohiko Kagawa, and dignitaries representing the
Baptist Mission in Japan. The gentle murmuring and stirring of
the audience hushed suddenly as Thomasine Allen entered the
room and was ushered to the platform. The program began with
introductory speeches, and two tiny kindergarten children came
forward almost obscured by a huge bouquet of flowers which
they solemnly presented to Miss Allen. Then the Governor of
Iwate Prefecture arose. He lifted a jeweled decoration from a
small, black lacquer box and turned to present it to Thomasine
Allen. From the accompanying scroll he read a proclamation:

> His majesty, the Emperor of Japan conferred on THOMASINE
> ALLEN, a citizen of the United States of America, the Fifth Order
> of Merit of the Sacred Jewel, and signed and sealed at the Imperial
> Palace on the 30th day of May in the 33rd year of Showa Era for
> the certification.

When the applause had died down, it was Tommy's turn to
speak and to acknowledge the honor she had received.

    This great honor should be shared by many people in the
United States and in Japan whose prayers and gifts of money
have made it possible to go forward, but it should be especially
shared by my mother, Lola Waggoner Allen, whose training in
our home in Franklin and whose decision to educate me in
Franklin College set my feet mission-ward, and by Mr. and
Mrs. Yahaba, who for many years have worked with me, and
whose vision, ability, and utter self-sacrifice have made this
work possible.

Chapter Two

THE WORLD FOR CHRIST IN THIS GENERATION

It is a long way from the plains of Indiana to the mountains of northeastern Japan, and it has been a long time since 1890, when Thomasine Allen was born in Franklin, Indiana.

Deep tragedy had marked the life of her mother, Lola Waggoner Allen, for her husband, Thomas Allen, had died of typhoid fever shortly before Tommy's birth. The little girl born to Lola Allen was small and not too strong; scarcely "one good bite for a cannibal," according to one neighbor. But the young widow and mother found hope and faith in her determination to make a good home for the new child and the older daughter, Marguerite. And she did make a good home for her children, for their childhood was delightfully happy even though it was fatherless.

Mrs. Allen bought a house in Franklin near Franklin College and rented rooms to the young college girls who came to attend the school. She worked hard and managed her money carefully so that the children were never really in want, and they enjoyed unusual educational and spiritual advantages by living in a pleasant middle western town on the campus of a small liberal arts college which was closely related to their church.

Straitened financial circumstances never discouraged Lola Allen from the support of her church, for it was most important to her. In the hall closet she kept a wallet into which she put ten percent of her income; and around the wallet, secured by a rubber band, was a paper marked, "The Lord's Purse." Occasionally, sudden needs forced her to borrow from the money she had set aside for a tithe, and, when this was necessary, she carefully noted, "Owe Lord's Purse 25c."

Family devotions were held each morning, and as soon as Tommy and Marguerite were old enough, they read from the Bible the verses with which the family started the day. As a beginning reader Tommy read the well-known verses about faith of such superior quality that it could move mountains. She decided to test this promise on the grass which grew so stubbornly between the bricks of the sidewalk. It was Tommy's job to pull out the grass, and in the hot Indiana summers it sprang up almost as quickly as she could tug it out. Settling herself on the back porch steps, she bowed her small head and prayed earnestly that the grass would be removed without her having to do the work. But when she opened her eyes to find the same green blades poking their way up between the red bricks, she began to realize that the removal of grass and the moving of mountains required both faith and human effort.

Close to the Allens lived many of the college faculty, among whom were scholars whose loyalty to Franklin College and to their students kept them from accepting more lucrative positions in other schools. On another occasion when Tommy was tugging at the tenacious green blades that had infiltrated the red bricks, Dr. William Taylor Stott, the college president, stopped to encourage her and to say, "Well, Thomasine, I used to have that job when I was a child." He went on his way, leaving behind the impression that perhaps, if she were faithful to the chore at hand, she, too, might grow up to become a college president!

Mrs. Allen's sturdy example of hard work and piety was strengthened by constant association with the college professional group, and regular attendance at prayer meeting left with Tommy a lasting impression of men who spoke each Wednesday night of what God had done for them during the week. And the wiggly little girl saw that these same devout professors put their faith into practice as they helped her widowed mother by cutting wood for the stove, mowing the lawn in summer time, and shoveling the heavy Indiana snows from the brick walks in winter time.

Vignettes of small-town life in late nineteenth-century America hold a nostalgic charm of their own for twentieth-century Americans. But what was there in Franklin that awakened a little girl's interest in far-off lands and sent her eventually into a poverty-stricken rural county in Japan; what influence went into the making of such a pioneer missionary? Surely it was that of Lola Waggoner Allen whom we have met briefly as a courageous young widow, faithfully tithing her meager income and supporting her two small daughters. She and her husband, before his untimely death, had dedicated their children to the service of the Lord, and Lola was determined that the children would be well prepared for his service. In later years a relative remarked to Tommy, "You didn't have a chance to be anything but a missionary; that was what you were brought up to be." And Tommy agreed, "It was, to some extent, simply the flowering of my mother's training."

There was also the atmosphere of the times; the last decades of the nineteenth century saw the United States awakening to the call of Manifest Destiny (a catchword that implied divine sanction for the territorial expansion of the young nation) and to the Great Missionary Crusade by its more devout citizens. At least two missionaries had been sent from Franklin before Tommy was born, and the town's interest had followed Judson Benjamin to Burma and Mary Thompson to Swatow, China. Franklin newspapers carried stories of happenings abroad, and readers learned about the background of the Empress of China as well as the agricultural practices in that exotic land, and breathlessly followed the explorations of Sir Henry M. Stanley in Africa. A strong religious tone colored even the newspapers, for the front pages of *The Democrat* were reserved for the sermons of the era's most famous preacher, Dewitt Talmadge. One of the great preachers who delighted congregations in the late nineteenth century, Talmadge was noted for his ability to select a biblical text and tailor its meaning to fit his immensely popular homilies. Week after week *The Democrat* printed his sermons for Franklin readers.

Two institutions were important to Tommy as a child and as a young woman. The First Baptist Church and Franklin College were so closely connected as to be almost intertwined, and in the realms of ethics and morals their teaching dovetailed. Students worshipped and studied in a remarkably consistent atmosphere of religious education, and this atmosphere provided by the church and college helped to influence Tommy in her life of mission.

Throughout the years of its history the Waggoners had played a leading role in the First Baptist Church. In 1881 Tommy's grandfather, Lycurgus Waggoner, was serving as a deacon and, along with the other deacons, was thus commended: "These all having performed the office of deacon well, have attained to a good degree and great boldness in the faith."[1] The boldness of Lycurgus Waggoner continued to live, for during all the years of growth of First Baptist Church and of Franklin College, whenever the cause of higher education was in doubt, the Waggoners always stood with the faction which believed in education. By the time Tommy was born, the community, the church, and the college were sharing the responsibility for training the young people of the town and had joined forces to provide the remarkably unified culture in which she and Marguerite grew to womanhood.

While Tommy was attending Franklin College from 1908 to 1911, the Student Volunteer Movement was riding high on a wave of enthusiasm which had originated in the Moody revivals during the 1870's and 1880's. Over 5,000 college and seminary students had enlisted as Student Volunteers by 1915.

Caught up in the idealistic ferment that was sweeping the colleges in the early 1900's, Tommy's older sister Marguerite volunteered for missionary service through the Student Volunteers. "Now," said her mother, "we must both pray that Tommy will make the same decision."

In Franklin the Student Volunteers met regularly for prayer and for study. Outside speakers came to present the needs of foreign countries and to urge the young men and women to become members of the association. Encouraged by her mother and by her sister's example, Tommy became a member. She knew that it was one of the happiest days of her mother's life.

[1] Dr. William T. Stott, *History of Fifty Years of the First Baptist Church.* Franklin, Ind., 1882, p. 16.

In that day the Student Volunteer Movement was very strong and largely under the leadership of John R. Mott, Sherwood Eddy, and Robert E. Speer. The slogan was, "Evangelize the world in this generation." We believed that if we all did our duty as we saw it, we *could* evangelize the world. It was a great motto. The fact that it was too big for what we could do was another matter; at least our ideals were up there.

Thus Tommy recalled the impact of a phenomenal collegiate movement. But even missionary saints are made and not born, and despite the piety of her home and school life, Tommy was enjoying herself. She was active in college activities and the YWCA, and was initiated into the social sorority, Pi Beta Phi.

However, Tommy found that her decision to volunteer for the foreign mission field had set her apart from the other students in the eyes of some of the churchmen and some of the professors. Naturally gay and sociable, and displaying even then the sense of humor which was to delight her friends through the years, she found that she was expected to conform to the missionary ideal held up before her by her mother, her sister, and some of her closest friends in the college.

 I loved dancing and card playing, but I noticed that it bothered my mother and also some of the professors. They felt distressed about it and thought I ought to be more of an example, that if I was going to be a foreign missionary I ought not to do these things. Of course this was part of the times in 1910. Christian sentiment at that time was opposed to things like that and in favor of a very strict observance of the Sabbath. After a great deal of thought and prayer, I decided that I would give up dancing and cards. It was hard — one of the hardest things I think I ever had to do, but at least it showed me that I could give something up and at the same time be happy.

After graduating from Franklin College in 1911, Tommy taught for a year in Albemarle, North Carolina, and then she enrolled at the Biblical Seminary in New York for additional study and preparation for mission service. Tommy later recalled her work in a New York settlement house which was part of the American Parish of the Presbyterian Church in the United States of America. Under the leadership of Dr. Norman Thomas, a leading exponent of the social gospel, the settlement house sponsored recreational and educational activities for the many new immigrants of the Upper East Side. Living in a world of violence, among newcomers from Italy, Hungary, and other eastern European nations, was a new experience for Tommy. After a childhood spent in the sheltered and pious atmosphere of rural Franklin, a new kind of education awaited her.

Even the playground contributed to Tommy's education, for she learned to watch for the older children who were given to threatening their juniors with knives when they wanted the swings. On one occasion Tommy tried to separate two fighting teenagers, and she saw the conflict grow into a battle that drew hundreds of parents and friends to the playground. However, she was not as afraid of the knives as of the cats that almost outnumbered the tenants of the crowded slum around the settlement house.

Two of the young Italian boys became Tommy's self-appointed guardians. Constantly they warned her of the perils of the East Side. "Don't you walk out alone at night, Miss Allen," they would say. "Any time you need to go any place we'll go with you. We'll protect you."

Tony and Walter knew whereof they spoke, for before their contact with the settlement house they had been skilled thieves. Tony liked to tell the story of one of his last hold-ups.

> You know what frisking is, don't you? We used to hold up people, and I would frisk the pockets and somebody else would hold the gun. One night in December I frisked a man's pockets and found ten dollars. The man said, "Oh, I was saving that money to buy Christmas presents for my children." I felt sorry about that, and I made the gang give the money back to him. I told them I would take them some place else. We went to another end of the park and held up another man and got one hundred dollars. "Now then," I told the gang, "I told you it paid to do right!"

Life in the American Parish was not all playground battles, knives, guns, and violence. Besides the playground the parish sponsored Boy Scout troops, Camp Fire Girls, Bible study, and clubs and meetings for adults. Many of the Italians attended a local Presbyterian church, coming in a group and sitting together. They brought to the services a zest for singing hymns that was long remembered by everyone who was connected with the American Parish.

It was a neighborhood house in every sense of the word. Work in the family and in the community was another stepping-stone and a great help in preparation for the mission field. When I got to Japan it was invaluable to know that missionary work was more than just teaching the Bible and working in a church that was already organized. What good is your religion if it doesn't change lives?

With college and seminary training now behind her and with some experience in teaching and in social work, Tommy was now ready for foreign service. She volunteered to meet with the Woman's American Baptist Foreign Mission Society which had recently been formed by the merger of several Baptist mission societies under the leadership of the dynamic Helen Barrett Montgomery.

 I didn't care what field, and I didn't even particularly care whether it was the foreign field or not. I was quite happy in the work among foreigners in the New York City settlement. I knew that there were many people who were more earnest Christians than I by far, but who could not go to the foreign field for various reasons. There was no reason why I could not go, and I felt that I must go where the need is greatest. I felt strongly even then, and this has been the guiding element in my life.

Once she had been accepted as a candidate by the Woman's American Baptist Foreign Mission Society, Tommy waited eagerly to know her assignment. Soon she learned that she was appointed to be the principal of the Sarah Curtis Home, a girls' school in Tokyo, Japan.

 Going to Japan in that day and generation was quite different from going any place today when the whole world has become one. One time I asked what kind of house I could expect to live in, and I was told that it would be an ordinary Japanese house. Of course, that didn't mean a thing to me because I had no idea what a Japanese house was like! Now people are so much better prepared for such a change in living, but then it was just a great big adventure, and we had no idea what we were facing.

Chapter Three

TO OUR TEACHER WHO HAS JUST COME

THOMASINE ALLEN WAS TWENTY-FIVE when, with a rapidly beating heart, she crossed the gangplank of the *Mongolia* and joined 250 other missionaries who were bound for the Orient. Most of them, like Tommy, were facing an unknown future, and during the long voyage they formed classes and discussion groups, clustering around the veteran missionaries who told them about the exotic lands that lay far to the west. Tommy was not much of a leader in those days, and only occasionally did her sense of humor bubble to the surface. She was quite content to play musical accompaniments while others performed. Eagerly she listened to what the old Japan hands could tell her about the country where she was to spend her life.

The empire which Tommy was approaching had isolated itself from foreign contacts for two hundred and fifty years. It was a challenge to nations that were interested in markets for their goods and in coaling stations for their steamships. Again and again western ships approached the shores of Japan to test the enforcement of her policy of isolation, but in 1854 Commodore Matthew C. Perry moored his Black Ships in the Yokohama harbor and broke the barrier that had secured Japan from all outside contacts. Before very long, trade treaties were signed with several western nations, and the first few foreigners moved into Japan.

The opening of the country resulted in a tremendous national upheaval. Yoshinobu Tokugawa, the last shogun, resigned, and the young Mutsuhito, later known as the Meiji Emperor, was enthroned, and he established his capital in Tokyo. Actual power of government shifted to a new group of de facto rulers, an oligarchy drawn largely from the young and gifted lower-ranking samurai. These brilliant Japanese leaders reduced the power and privileges of feudal lords and warring rulers. Then they reorganized the nation into political units of prefectures and counties, built a modern army and navy, and established a system of universal public education which reached into every hamlet and cove of the islands. Through all this they fought the Chinese to a standstill in 1895, defeated the Russian Empire in 1905, and managed all of these changes without disrupting the basic stability of the nation.

When the Meiji Emperor died in 1912, he left behind him a nation which had moved in less than fifty years from the Elizabethan world into the twentieth century. Internationally, Japan was accepted on an almost equal basis by the family of nations and was regarded as well qualified to defend herself from aggression. Internally, Japan was well on its way to industrialization and possessed a constitution which provided the machinery for parliamentary government. The Meiji reformers had achieved many of their goals; they had transformed the nation, but all of the reforms were effected from the top down. Even the constitution, the courts, and the Diet were regarded as gifts to the people, and there was no question as to the supremacy of the executive power exercised in the name of the Emperor.

At this time Japan was allied with England in foreign affairs, and, as an ally, supported the cause of the English in their war with the Central Powers. In 1915 Japan took the opportunity to extend her influence in China, issuing demands on the government which the Chinese refused to consider, and which brought reproofs from the United States and Great Britain. When the United States government protested, Japan quoted the Monroe Doctrine and suggested that she was justified in applying a similar doctrine in China. Count Okuma urged the Diet to pass the budget of 620 million yen which included 100 million yen for the Navy and a sizable sum for the Army.

Japanese business was prospering. The president of the Yokohama Specie Bank, Mr. Inouye, told his shareholders that the advance in exports so favorable to Japan had been caused by the export of war necessities to friendly powers, the recovery of American financial circles from depressed conditions, and the increase in the market for Japanese goods in India, Australia, and the South Seas, where the import of European goods had largely been suspended.

But Viscount Kentaro Kaneko, diplomat and friend of President Theodore Roosevelt, looked at the European war with the eyes of a humanitarian. He expressed the belief that the experiences of the war had been so bitter that when peace came, the European nations would be morally and economically compelled to devise some means of international cooperation which would prevent a recurrence of bloodshed and destruction.

Tommy was familiar with the historical background of Japan, and from her fellow passengers she gained impressions of its current status. As they talked, the old missionaries assured the newcomers that Christianity was well established in Japan and, although numerically small, it was recognized by the government as one of the national religions. This recognition was made official when Christians were invited to participate in the Three Religions Conference held in 1912, and it was reinforced when Dr. Michio Kozaki, president of the Federation of Churches, represented Protestantism at a dinner in commemoration of the enthronement. Imperial honors were conferred upon fourteen outstanding educators as part of the celebration, and seven of these were Christians.

At last the long voyage to Japan was over, and the *Mongolia* entered Yokohama Harbor. Eager passengers lined the rails for a glimpse of towering Mount Fuji and their first sight of the waterfront buildings, and fellow missionaries came aboard the ship to greet the newcomers. Dr. John L. Dearing, Mr. J. F. Gressitt, and Miss Minnie Carpenter, members of the Japan Baptist Mission, were on hand to meet Tommy and welcome her to Japan. The ship docked on Sunday, and Miss Carpenter explained quietly, "We're not going up to Tokyo now. We can't let the girls see that we travel on Sunday, so we'll stay all night in Yokohama and go to Tokyo tomorrow. We have to keep the Sabbath." Tommy spent her first night in Japan as the guest of the wife of an American businessman. She described their home on the bluff as "an Oriental dream."

Monday morning they took the train to Tokyo, and, as they crossed the few miles of farm land separating the two cities, the girl from Indiana saw for the first time the neatly laid-out fields, the tiny grey houses, and the people — people of another race, background, and world. Once consular formalities were concluded and she was settled in Tokyo, Tommy had time to reflect on her first impressions. "The people are so tiny, and the houses look quite like doll houses; I'm about twice too tall. I took a jinrikisha up to the school, and it seems quite inhuman to be pulled by one of those tiny men."

Tommy's new home was a pleasant room in a house which was a combination of Japanese and foreign architecture. As soon as she had unpacked and put her belongings away, she received a gracious welcome from her colleague, Miss Antoinette Whitman. Tommy said later, "No new missionary could have had a better example and ideal set before her than Miss Whitman. She was a perfect lady; gentle, firm, and gracious in all her ways — a Christian gentlewoman." And as Tommy met the fifty young girls who were living and studying in the high school, she remarked, "So very polite, I couldn't get over it; all the bowing and scraping were new to me."

The girls invited her to a party being given in her honor, and for the first time Tommy knelt on tatami-covered floors and settled back on her heels to watch the entertainment. Two of the girls, speaking in formal and careful English, welcomed her on behalf of the student body and urged her to stay forever. Then the entire group joined in the welcome song:

> To our teacher who has just come:
> In this school where the flowers blossom and the birds are singing,
> After receiving your instruction we shall strive to be diligent,
> Holding on to your sleeves.
>
> To our teacher whom we welcome today:
> Tho' we are like cherry trees we shall bathe in the dew
> Of thy blessings till we, growing stronger and stronger,
> Shall become pillars in the Kingdom of God.

After the welcoming song the girls repeated Psalm 100 and bowed their heads for prayer. Then two serious young girls glided forward to present a bouquet of flowers to the new teacher with many deep bows, and the formal part of the program came to an end. Now the girls and their new teacher could relax and enjoy koto and samisen music, humorous dialogues, and tableaux. Japanese tea was served in delicate porcelain bowls, and sweet cakes were passed to mark the end of the party.

Although Tommy lived at the school for the first two years, her work with the students was limited to casual contacts and to playing games with them after her stint at the Japanese language school. "Skip To My Lou" and "London Bridge Is Falling Down" provided pleasant opportunities for the girls to practice English and supplied needed recreation for their teacher, who had now become a student herself.

 We had lots of fun in language school, for all of us were grown people who had had some experience in life; yet we were all just little kindergarten children learning to say, "What is this? It is a book. It is a clock." We had good times there as we kept all of the American holidays, all of the British holidays, and all of the Japanese holidays. In the meantime, we studied Japanese!

Of course I went to the Japanese church, and I often played the organ at some of the services. On one of the first Sundays I heard the pastor repeating my name all through his sermon. *Thomasine* is pronounced *tamashii* in Japanese, and every other sentence had *tamashii* in it. I wondered how on earth he knew my name, and why he was talking about me. Finally, I located my language teacher in the church, and I asked her, "Why are they talking about me? They don't know me! What is that word?" She explained that *tamashii* is the word that means soul, and, of course, it was quite right and proper that the pastor should be talking about the soul!

Other missionaries had had such problems, too.

Miss Mary Jessie, with whom I lived in Sendai, was quite disturbed one Sunday because she thought the pastor was insisting that even cats can be saved. Actually he was talking about Nicodemus, but Nicodemus pronounced in Japanese is *nekodemo* which means "even cats." Miss Jessie was sure there was something wrong with the pastor's theology since he kept saying that even cats can be saved!

Tommy's first two years in Japan passed quickly and happily, and she found herself fitting naturally into the Japanese scene. She could kneel on the floor as gracefully as her students, and the niceties of Japanese etiquette were becoming second nature to her. The girls, who dressed formally in kimono and *hakama* — Japanese pleated skirts, no longer looked strange to her. They in turn were losing their initial shyness and becoming Tommy's fast friends. She looked forward now to passing the language examinations and taking up her teaching duties.

But the fellowship she enjoyed with the girls and the other teachers and the fun of learning a new language were not the only meaningful experiences of those early years. As Tommy began to meet some of the senior missionaries, she learned that the problems of the church in the Orient were very real and quite often vexing.

The mission was feeling the pinch of finances and felt that it was impossible to keep up four girls' schools in Japan. One school had to be closed, and the Sarah Curtis Home was chosen. Tommy was transferred to the Shokei Girls School in Sendai, north of Tokyo. Then, after the sad business of closing the school, she bade farewell to the girls and to her language school classmates and boarded the train for Sendai.

Chapter Four

CITY OF THE STAR FESTIVAL

NORTHWARD BOUND FROM UENO STATION, the train carried Tommy toward a new city, new friends, and, eventually, toward a new life. Sendai was a pleasant and spacious town, free from the bustle of the hurried capital with its maze of crooked, crowded streets. As an educational center, Sendai was the site of the Tohoku Imperial University and of several mission schools: Tohoku Gakuin, a college for young men, and Miyagi Jo Gakko and Shokei Jo Gakuin, for young women.

On the seventh day of the seventh month of each year, Sendai blossoms with bamboo branches covered with strips of brightly colored paper. Each piece of paper bears a Japanese poem of love, and under the bamboo branches are lacquer stands with food offerings. Citizens of Sendai delight in the celebration of Tanabata, the Star Festival. According to an ancient Chinese legend, two stars, the Herdsman and the Weaving Girl, fell in love. They loved each other so deeply that they left their work, allowing the cattle to stray from their pastures and the looms to become dusty and neglected. Because they were so careless of their duties, the two lovers were punished by separation; they were banished to opposite sides of the Celestial River, or Milky Way. But the Lord of High Heaven took pity on their sad and lonely exile and decreed that they might visit each other once a year. So, on the night of the seventh day of the seventh moon, the Herdsman and the Weaving Girl are reunited in the skies above Sendai, and the city is made gay with bamboo branches and strips of paper covered with love poems.

Although Tommy was accustomed to a strict way of life in her own family and the equally austere regimen which had prevailed at the Sarah Curtis Home, she was not prepared for the atmosphere of Shokei Jo Gakuin in Sendai. The school was dominated by the principal, Miss Annie Buzzell.

 She was a very, very Spartan individual, always wearing long skirts and men's Congress boots, and her hair was pulled back very tightly. Her training was equally severe, and it was hard for the students; and it was just as hard for the other missionaries, especially for me, the only young person out from America. Miss Buzzell was a real pioneer who had known some mighty hard days in her home in Nebraska, days in which grasshoppers had eaten up the entire crop.

Miss Buzzell was, indeed, a real pioneer woman. Born in 1866, in Lowell, Massachusetts, she grew up in the frontier territory of Nebraska. Here her father served as a home missionary, working to civilize the rough and ready pioneer settlements. Annie arrived in Japan in 1892 and went directly to the new girls' school in Sendai where she stayed for twenty-seven years, serving for twenty years as the principal of the school. When she left Shokei, in 1920, she moved to a small village, Tono, and began evangelistic work among the women and children of the community. Although retired, Miss Buzzell continued her activities until 1935; then she returned to Sendai and lived there quietly until her death in 1936. At the many memorial services, one Bible verse was invariably quoted: "My Father is working still, and I am working" (John 5:17 RSV).

Certainly Annie Buzzell worked hard during her years at Shokei: She was the first one up in the morning, and immediately on arising she toured the school. She checked every detail, from the amount of coal being used in the stove to the condition of the playground. After the inspection tour, she aroused the girls for exercises, an early breakfast, and lengthy devotions. Nothing escaped her attention, and it was not long before the matter of suitable dress arose between the stern and dedicated principal in the Congress boots and the new young teacher.

 Her clothes were so old-fashioned, and here I came fresh out of college with georgette blouses, shorter skirts, and, worst of all, silk stockings. The girls got a great kick out of me, not only

because I was so different in age but also different in dress. Once
Miss Buzzell said to me, "Can't you settle down and put on
cotton hose? You'll freeze to death!" Well, I soon found out that
I was freezing to death, and I put my pride out a little bit!

After the departure of Miss Buzzell in 1920, Shokei proved an
easier place to work, and Tommy stayed there for ten years
teaching English and Bible classes in the school and working
with women and children in the churches. For a time she
thoroughly enjoyed the social and intellectual life of the area,
for Sendai was headquarters for most of the mission work in
the north and had a sizable foreign colony.

While she lived in Sendai, Tommy assisted in the work in
the small churches which had been established in some of the
nearby villages. The first Baptist missionary in the north was
the Reverend T. P. Poate, Professor of English at Tokyo University and a British subject. Mr. Poate wandered throughout
the northern provinces on foot, by jinrikisha, and by boat, preaching to all who would listen and organizing his converts into
churches. In 1889 he was joined by the Reverend Mr. R. L.
Halsey and Mrs. Halsey, both teachers. But a reaction against
foreigners and against Christianity marked the last decade of
the nineteenth century. Suspicion and hostility were very pronounced in the rural areas, and little progress was possible.
Nevertheless, there were Christians who held to their faith, and
some of the little churches near Sendai survived.

Tommy was now living on the Christian frontier, for north
of Sendai there were no mission schools such as Shokei, and
only a few churches were to be found in the larger towns. She
was also becoming familiar with the paradoxical character of
the Janus-like Japanese villager who was his nation's most conservative, and (at the same time) its most revolutionary citizen.
As she talked with the country women and taught the country
children, Tommy began to wonder if teaching school in Sendai
was right for her as a missionary when there stretched a land
to the north where there was almost no Christian work or influence. Slowly the problems of this needy area began to demand
her attention and concern.

During the 1920's, there were two distinct branches of the

Christian movement in Japan. Although the Japanese church was small, it was securely established. But it had lost the zeal of its early days and was content to abide within its own walls, baptizing its own children and bringing them up to stand apart from the wider community. The church was strongly influenced by the theology of the conservative Dr. Tokutaro Takakura, president of the Presbyterian seminary, *the Tokyo Shingakusha Shingakko,* and pastor of one of the largest churches in Tokyo. Dr. Takakura's theology was involved with the church, the gospel, and the faith, but it was not concerned with social service, moral activity, or satisfying religious moods.[2]

However, the creative movements of Christianity were carried on apart from the organized churches. High-minded non-Christian Japanese were active in agencies of moral and social reform, and they welcomed Christian participation in their efforts to solve the problems facing the newly-industrialized nation. The most notable exponent of the Japanese social gospel was Dr. Toyohiko Kagawa whose book, *Crossing the Death Line,* opened the eyes of the nation to the wretched conditions in its industrial slums. Christians were active in the peace movement and in temperance and anti-prostitution organizations. They advocated fair labor laws and did social work among the laboring classes. The Japanese social gospel was characterized by a vital and creative relevance to Japanese society, but it was often characterized by a tendency to compromise.

Church membership was concentrated in the large cities. Such members as moved to the country found it almost impossible to maintain their faith in the hostile rural atmosphere, and there were few rural churches to provide any strengthening fellowship. Japanese and missionary sociologists, aware of the urban concentration of the church, undertook studies and surveys of rural life. "What," they asked, "are the spiritual needs of the farmers and fishermen, and what sort of church would meet these men and women on their own ground?" Suggestions

[2] Charles Hugh Germany, "Dominant Theological Currents in Japanese Protestant Christianity from 1920 to 1958 with Particular Reference to the Nature of Their Understanding of the Responsibility of the Christian to Society" (unpublished Ph.D. dissertation). New York: Columbia University, 1959, p. 158.

and recommendations came from discussions and consultations, but there were few Christians eager to live in the country and test the conclusions.

As the needs of the country people became real to Tommy, her restlessness and dissatisfaction grew. She was becoming bored with the routine of teaching gentle, docile Japanese school girls and with the modest round of social life in Sendai. She could not believe that a life spent in the stifling school atmosphere was for her an effective response to the Great Commission. Moreover, she could not close her mind to the picture of thousands of men and women facing serious social and religious problems without anyone to suggest to them a better way of life.

 I finally decided that it was better for me to leave Sendai. Many missionaries were willing to go there and teach English and do routine work as their calling, but I had become acquainted with country work and it interested me very much. As someone said, I was well-qualified for country work because I had no sense of smell, a gift of gab, and I liked Japanese food. Those were my three qualifications! Anyway, I did have those qualities; I liked the country work, I liked the country people, and I liked the country food.

Every experience brings something of real value to us, and one of the greatest things I got out of Sendai was Kuni Obara. She was in the fifth year when I came, and I could see that she was different. All the other girls came crowding around this new young foreigner to see what I was like, but not Kuni; she would run when she saw me coming. I thought, "Here is a girl who is different; she has a mind of her own, and she doesn't follow the herd." I think that was the thing that made her stand out for me and made her seem so special.

Kuni Obara was born in a little village in Iwate Ken, the oldest of three sisters. Her father was an invalid, and she did not have an easy childhood, but the moral standards of the family were high and true to the best of the Japanese tradition. She says of her childhood:

My home was not a Christian home, but my father was very particular in rearing us, and so was my mother. They tried to instill in our hearts the idea that we must be useful to other people, that we should not be selfish and think only of ourselves, and that we should consider our neighbors and our community, and do all we could for them. For this I have always been very grateful.

There was a Holiness Church in the town where Kuni lived, and she attended Sunday school and learned a little about Christianity there. As she grew up, her parents hoped that she would attend a normal school and become a teacher. Then her uncle, the Reverend Mr. Tomojiro Obara, pastor of a Holiness Church in Yodobashi, Tokyo, urged her parents to send Kuni to a mission school. There, he felt, she would learn the things necessary for a life of service.

Taking the advice of her uncle, Kuni Obara entered Shokei. Quiet and reserved, she submitted gracefully to the stern discipline of Miss Buzzell's regime and kept her own counsel; but, when Tommy came to Shokei, Kuni felt as though someone had pushed back the wooden shutters to reveal a spring-morning world of sunshine, blue sky, and flowers. However, Kuni was not one to rush to the open window or to race out into the garden. Her reserve had to be overcome very gradually, and her friendship was slowly won. At last confidence and trust were established, and Tommy could say to her what she had long felt to be true. Even as she spoke, Tommy was years ahead of her time in her concept of mission: 1289023

 I am a missionary, but there will always be many things that I cannot do, things that the Japanese will have to do, and I would like to be able to count on you, Kuni. I think you are the one to carry on.

Once Kuni had accepted Tommy's friendship and the goal of Christian service, she determined to do all that she could to prepare herself for this new life. After a year of study at the Women's Bible Training School in Osaka, she returned to Shokei to teach and to assist Tommy. At this time, Thomasine Allen was teaching a course on the Old Testament, and she needed Kuni's help in preparing the lectures. Kuni also participated in the work with women and children in the little churches near Sendai, and the qualities of leadership that Tommy had seen in her began to develop and grow.

Before the Meiji Restoration in 1868, Confucian traditions dominated Japanese educational thought, and women had little opportunity for higher education. Christian churches pioneered in this field, and Ferris School for girls was the first Christian school for women in Japan. At the time of Kuni's graduation a high school diploma was an unusual achievement for a Japanese girl, and very few ever considered college training. However, Kuni felt that she should continue her education, so she decided to resign her position as an instructor in the high school and enroll in the newly-opened junior college of Shokei. She told Tommy:

> Sensei, if we're going to do effective Christian work, we Japanese women must have more education. Up to now a high school diploma was enough, but in the future it's not going to be that way. We will have to have a college education. And so, I have decided to resign as your helper. I want to take the three-year course in the junior college.

Kuni gave up her position as a teacher and joined the students she had formerly taught. She earned her junior college degree in 1925, and after graduation she accompanied Tommy to the United States to be enrolled as a junior at Franklin College.

On the journey to America they visited the Bible lands, for Tommy felt that a knowledge of the sights and scenes of the Scriptures would be of great value in Kuni's future work of teaching the Bible.

I remember one man on the boat saying, "Why in the world do you want to go to Palestine? It's so dirty you couldn't pay me to go there." When I told him that the purpose of our trip was to see this land, he nearly fell overboard.

We wouldn't have missed the trip to Palestine for anything, but with the events that have happened since, I am particularly glad that we did take it at that time. Of course, we were most interested in the outdoor things that are truly authentic like the wells of water. You feel that when there is a well, it really *is* the place mentioned in the Bible. But the other things, which have churches built over them, are interesting only traditionally. The worship that millions of people have paid to these places, whether they are authentic or not, is another matter.

We left the ship at Suez and took the train north, and the first thing I saw was Gaza — Samson's Gaza. However, one of my greatest thrills was to see the station with the sign "Jerusalem." This had always been just a Bible word, but now it was real. We stayed at the YWCA and went with Arab guides to the Wailing Wall and to other traditional places such as Bethlehem, Nazareth, Capernaum, and the Sea of Galilee. The whole trip meant so much, especially to Kuni.

When they reached the United States, Kuni settled down at Franklin College and found a warm welcome from Tommy's friends in the church, the college, and the town itself. It was not easy for her to make the transition from Japanese society to the entirely different ways of American life, but she did well in her college classes and was able to complete her work at Franklin in two years. Then she went to New York University where she earned a Master of Arts degree in Religious Education. Looking back on her experiences in the United States, Kuni said:

> Two things stand out in my memory: I was never treated as a foreigner. The Americans were all kind to me and took me in as one of their number, so I felt right at home. I never felt that I was a foreigner in their midst. Another thing which impressed me greatly was the Christian home and the beautiful education that the American young people had from childhood on. There was nothing like it that I knew in Japan — nothing like those wonderful Christian homes in which I was a guest so many, many times.

Kuni's impressions of America were most favorable.

Chapter Five

THERE ARE MANY ROADS

TOMMY, TOO, WENT BACK TO SCHOOL. She enrolled in the Graduate School of the University of Chicago to do some work in comparative religions. Soon she found that some of her friends thought that advanced training was a waste of time for anyone interested in working in the country.

Many people in America said to me, "If you are going into country work, why in the world do you want an M.A.? You don't need a Master's degree for work up there." Well, you don't, in a way. But I felt that the country needed just as much as the city; no chain is stronger than its weakest link. The northern rural areas were very backward, and if we could raise their level, then the whole chain of Japan would be stronger. I felt that way all along, and so did Kuni.

The University of Chicago was a private, nonsectarian university, although the Baptist layman, Mr. John D. Rockefeller, had given generously to the school, and the charter provided that thirty percent of the trustees must be Baptists. It was a stimulating and challenging intellectual climate which Tommy found in the Graduate School. Dr. Shailer Matthews was dean of the Divinity School; Dr. Edgar Goodspeed was engaged in the translation work which was to bring him unexpected fame and a certain amount of controversy; and Dr. Theodore Soares and Dr. A. Eustace Hayden were teaching religious education.

The courses on comparative religions were especially helpful to me because they offered me the opportunity to delve deeper into the religions of Japan and into the religions of other countries related to Japan. Under Dr. Hayden I wrote my thesis,

Religious Educational Values of Japanese Folklore. It demanded a great deal of reading and research, and that was all very beneficial and helpful to me in my work in the years to come.

Tommy discovered that the many religions of Japan are often compared to the roads leading toward the summit of a mountain; no matter which road the traveler chooses to follow, the ultimate destination of all is the same. The Japanese have indeed followed many roads, highways which have often crossed one another or run along parallel lines. At times they have merged completely, only to become separate branches on another part of the mountain.

Shinto, Buddhism, and Confucianism blend to form the faith of Japan. Tanaka San, Japan's "Mr. Smith," goes to the Shinto shrine on New Year's Day. Dressed in his best suit or in formal kimono, he walks beneath the torii and washes his hands to purify himself. At the god-house he makes an offering and bows his head, because he is Japanese and Shinto is the religion of Japan. But when his father dies, Tanaka San calls the Buddhist priest to perform the funeral service, and an elaborately gilded hearse carries his father's ashes to a Buddhist cemetery, because the Tanaka family belongs to a Buddhist sect. He calls on his family for sacrifices in order that his older son may go to college, and he speaks to his employer with honorific words because his ethical training has been Confucian.

This blending of religious ideas and beliefs came not only from the folklore of the land, but from the political and philosophical history of the past fifteen hundred years. Sometime in the sixth century Buddhism was first taught in Japan.

When the king of one of the Korean kingdoms sent gifts to the Japanese Court, he included Buddhist sutras and a gold-plated image, the forerunner of the thousands of Buddhas, Bodhisattvas, and Kwannons that now blanket Japan. The new religion, highly recommended by the Korean king, was received with reserve, but one of the important court families, the Soga, was given custody of the image and ordered to perform the prescribed worship as a test of the Buddha's power. Shortly thereafter a plague broke out, obviously indicating the native gods' disapproval, and the image was thrown into the river.

Despite this initial setback, Buddhism appealed strongly to many of the court families, and a struggle began between the pro-Buddhist faction and the champions of national beliefs. Finally the pro-Buddhists triumphed, placed the Empress Suiko on the throne, and made her gifted nephew, Prince Shotoku, the prince regent. In his seventeen-article constitution the prince enjoined his subjects, "Revere sincerely the three treasures — Buddha, the law, and the order — for these are the supreme objects of faith in all countries." In the Nara period, a golden age for Buddhism, magnificent temples and works of art were built in the city of Nara, then the capital of Japan. Court families competed in adorning Nara with religious magnificence.

But imperial patronage and court favor had an adverse affect on the Nara Buddhists; as they gained wealth and political power, they became corrupt and dissipated their spiritual vitality. In A.D. 794, the capital was transferred to the city of Kyoto, largely to enable the court to escape from the meddling and intimidation of the priests and monks. The Emperor, who was concerned over the decline of Buddhism, dispatched two priests to China in 805, hoping that their studies abroad would help to bring about a reformation of Japanese Buddhism. These two remarkable leaders, Saicho and Kukai, introduced into Japan the Tendai school of Buddhism, which quite lived up to the Emperor's hopes.

Tendai philosophy, as the two emissaries taught it on their return, included four major tenets which became the basis for Japanese Buddhism and influenced all future Japanese religious thought. First of all, there was the doctrine of universal salvation which broke the barrier that had previously set Buddhism apart as a religion only for the elite. Then, there were elaborate esoteric practices which, if pursued by the faithful, carried the promise of worldly well-being; and these, too, had widespread appeal. A most important Tendai innovation for Japan was a system for merging the two pantheons of Buddhism and Shinto. Shintoists, who already accepted the most extensive pantheon in the entire history of religion, perhaps, simply included Buddhist deities and assigned them to their proper functions. The Buddhists took another view of the problem; their solution was to see Shinto deities as derivative manifestations of the Buddhist deities. This merger solved many philosophical problems and made possible the dual religious allegiance which many Japanese found congenial.

Warriors of the Tokugawa period (1603-1868) combined Zen Buddhism with the philosophy of the Chinese Confucianist, Chu Hsi. These ideas provided the foundation for the moral code called Bushido. Never an organized religion or a sect, Bushido was a moral atmosphere in which loyalty was the highest virtue. Most of the great stories of Japanese literature extol sacrificial loyalty or probe agonizing conflicts of different loyalties.

The Meiji leaders, who replaced the shogunate in 1868, found themselves leading a nation which did not have a really firm religious foundation. At first they tried to restore Shinto as a national religion, but the naive beliefs and historical absurdities of Shinto were not acceptable to a nation now exposed to a wealth of knowledge from the outside world.

Shinto myths tell of the creation of Japan by the two gods, Izanagi and Izanami, who stood on a bridge from the Plain of High Heaven and dipped a celestial spear into the waters. From the spear fell drops of water and these drops became the islands of Japan. The sun goddess, Amaterasu-omikami, sent her grandson to rule over the country, and his great grandson, Jimmu Tenno, was the first emperor. Jimmu Tenno received from the gods three tokens of authority: a mirror, a jewel, and a sword; symbols of the sun, the moon, and the lightning. Amaterasu was the deity of the Yamato clan which dominated southern Japan in the early centuries of the Christian era, and, as the fortunes of the Yamato clan rose, she moved into a position of primary importance in the Japanese pantheon. The myth of the celestial solar ancestress was used by the authors of the eighth century chronicles, the *Kojiki* and the *Nihon Shoki,* to emphasize the national authority of the Court. Its legends and stories color Japanese art, literature, music, and drama much as biblical themes and stories color the expressions of western culture.

Count Shigenobu Okuma, one of the great Meiji leaders, noted that Restoration Shinto was a dismal failure because, while everyone talked about it, nobody actually believed in it. The next alternative which suggested itself to the national planners was the construction of what was called Daikyo, "the Great Religion." It had a simple creed with three doctrines: to embody respect for the gods and love for Japan, to preach "heavenly reason" and "the way of humanity," and to revere the Emperor and obey the authorities. It was no more successful than Restoration Shinto.

The search for an ideology which would unify the nation went on, and then the national planners found the solution which they were seeking. Shinto, said the government, was not a religion at all, but a reverent patriotism in which all true Japanese could participate, no matter what other religion they might profess. The architects of state Shinto borrowed an ethical framework from the largely Confucian Bushido or Code of the Warrior, set up an elaborate hierarchy of national shrines, and placed the Emperor on the pinnacle of their structure. They regarded their handiwork and found it good, and it required a cataclysmic war to topple the structure into the dust.

While the philosophers in the monasteries studied and dreamed and the politicians planned, millions of Japanese lived in a world dominated by a pantheistic feeling for nature and by primitive religious concepts. Tommy knew that the north was not a land of magnificent shrines and temples, nor of great monasteries and universities. In rural Japan the traditional rites that related to agriculture were important; harmony with nature was the goal of the farmer, and he performed the rituals as a matter of course, just as he mended the dikes and watered the fields. Superstitions, beliefs in omens, lucky days, and lucky directions, and faith in shamanism were all a part of village religious life. There was no easy answer to the question, *what does the common man believe?* But there were keys in the legends and stories that the people told and loved, and Tommy turned to a careful study of Japanese folklore for her thesis. One authority had said, "The north has no history, only legends." Here she hoped to get an idea of the values and goals of the people with whom she proposed to spend the rest of her life.

In the charming story, "The Knight Who Was Restored to His Estate," Tommy found many of the ideal virtues of the feudal code which structured Japanese life. Here is how she retells it:

Many years ago there lived a famous Regent by the name of Tokoyori, a wise and just ruler who was concerned for his people. He knew he could not always believe his advisers, so he resigned and turned the regency over to his son. Disguising himself as a mendicant priest, he set out to travel through the towns and villages to see the real condition of his people.

One night, in the midst of winter, he lost his way and was overtaken by a heavy snowstorm. He struggled on through the drifts and bent his head into the bitter wind, but he began to fear that he would freeze to death before he could reach shelter. Just as he was almost at the point of despair, he saw a small hut in the midst of the trees, and he staggered to the door. The humble couple who opened the door welcomed him, and as he sat near their tiny fire and drank their hot tea, he realized that his life had been saved.

Said his host, "I am a very poor farmer, as you can see, and I cannot offer you a good meal, but to our simple fare you are very welcome."

The disguised priest bowed low and said he was most thankful for their kindness, for he had walked all day long without tasting any food. There was no rice in his bowl, only millet, and the coarse fare was a novelty to a man accustomed to the delicacies of the palace. But he ate hungrily and found both hunger and hospitality worthy spices.

After supper they all sat around the hearth talking. The room became colder as they talked, for the storm still raged, and the little fire burned very low. The farmer turned to the fuel box, but it was empty of either wood or charcoal. Excusing himself, he stepped out into the snow-covered garden and returned with three pots of beautiful dwarfed trees. One was a plum, one a cherry, and the other a pine. With the eye of an expert the priest noted that the trees were of great age and value.

"On such a winter night as this," said the farmer, "a good fire is the only thing with which you can entertain a traveler. I will burn these trees to warm you before you retire."

"No," exclaimed the astonished guest, "these trees are beautifully trained; you must not burn them for me!"

"Never mind, my reverend guest," said the farmer breaking the trees and putting them on the fire, and as he watched the flame he seemed to be absorbed in thought. Then he spoke again: "True, once the plum used to teach me purity of heart and forebearance in hardship, for it blooms in early spring, even amidst the snow; and the cherry often inspired me with the spirit of a knight, for though it blossoms in splendor, it does not grudge its end in a night's storm any more than does the gallant soldier who offers his life for the country and the Emperor; and the evergreen pine gave noble lessons in the fidelity of the soul in the presence of prosperity and in adversity. But now, goodbye to you, old friends. If you could speak, I am sure you would say how pleased you are to be used to serve the comfort of my guest."

Tokoyori smiled as he heard these words, and he said to his host, "I recognize in you the breeding of a samurai. Will you not tell me your real name?"

At first his host would not reply, but at last he said, "I am a samurai and my name is Tsuneyo," and he went on to tell how he had been ruined through the dishonesty of an unworthy relative. Then he ended: "It was partly through my own neglect, however, that I was reduced to this condition, and I would rather amend my fault by illustrious deeds than by resorting to law. Should war break out and a call to arms be sounded, I shall be the first to Kamakura, wearing my torn armor, carrying my rusty sword, and riding my emaciated horse; and I will do glorious deeds once more!"

As they talked the night passed, and the day began to break; Tokoyori rose to depart. When the farmer and his wife came to the door to see him off, the Regent said, "Remember my words; I take leave with the firm belief that fate will give us the pleasure of meeting again some day."

The next spring the government at Kamakura issued an order calling upon all samurai to present themselves in battle array before the Regent. Tsuneyo had no money to buy a new suit of armor or to purchase a good steed, but he set off at once for Kamakura in his shabby outfit, and he rode day and night on his one horse. As he rode in amongst the well-equipped warriors, they laughed at his appearance and scoffed at him. But he drew himself up proudly and rode through their ranks with dignity; he knew that they had lost the true samurai spirit because they boasted of their appearance, while he, though shabbily clothed and poorly mounted, could surpass them in courage and loyalty.

There was a stir in the crowd of warriors, and soon a herald made his way through them calling, "The Regent summons to his presence the knight who wears the shabbiest armor and who rides the poorest horse."

"The Regent is going to punish me for daring to appear in this miserable state," said Tsuneyo to himself, "but to obey the summons is my duty." So with a heavy heart but with his head held high, he rode through the jeering crowd and followed the herald to the palace of the Regent.

Inside he prostrated himself before the young Regent, waiting for the condemnation he was sure to receive. Instead he heard the young man ask, "Are you the Knight Tsuneyo? I wish to present you to my father." A retainer pushed open the screens of an inner room, and there was Tokoyori magnificently dressed in his robes of office. An exclamation of surprise burst from the lips of Tsuneyo as he recognized in the great personage the humble priest whom he had sheltered in his cottage the year before.

"Oh," exclaimed Tsuneyo, "forgive my rudeness to you that night. I did not know who my guest was!"

The Regent spoke solemnly. "It is for me to thank you for all of the kindness you showed on that occasion. Had it not been for your hospitality, I should not be alive today. Do you think I have forgotten that you burned your precious dwarfed trees that cold night for my comfort? The glow of that fire has remained in my heart to this day!

"As an expression of my gratitude, I am going to give you, in addition to the territory you lost through your unworthy kinsman, the village of Matsueda in return for the *matsu* (pine tree); the village of Umeda in place of the *ume* (plum tree); and the village of Sakurai in return for the *sakura* (cherry tree)." Tsuneyo could not speak, for tears arose to his eyes and sobs of joy choked his heart.

The news of his reward was quickly spread, and the men who had laughed at him before bowed respectfully now as he passed along the ranks. Tsuneyo won the esteem of all the people because of his qualities of the true samurai, and they rejoiced at the just reward he had received for his loyalty, bravery, and kindness.

Chapter Six

CASTLE TOWN ON THE FRONTIER

AFTER TOMMY FINISHED HER STUDIES and received her degree, in 1929, she set sail again for Japan. Now she felt as though she was on the way home, for chatter of the Japanese sailors was familiar and comprehensible, and the customs which had seemed so strange in 1915 were ways to which she now conformed easily and naturally. And, she hoped, she was returning with a heightened understanding of the ideas and values that undergirded the structure of Japanese life. As the wake of the ship lengthened and disappeared on the eastern horizon, Tommy found herself looking forward to the adventure of life in a new city and to greater independence than she had known before. She was to be transferred from the Shokei Girls School in Sendai to Morioka, a castle town and the capital of Iwate Prefecture. Relieved of teaching responsibilities, she knew she would be free to work in the churches near Morioka, and she hoped to establish a neighborhood center in a community where there was no church.

In Morioka, for the first time, Tommy was faced with living in a Japanese house, cooking in a Japanese kitchen, and trying to keep warm with Japanese charcoal fire pots. The Japanese house is basically a framework fitted with sliding doors and shutters, and the floors are covered with rice straw matting or *tatami*. Dark and dirty kitchens were the rule, and Tommy did more scrubbing than evangelizing during her first months in Morioka. She learned to use charcoal for cooking and managed to do some baking in a small oven placed on top of the charcoal, but she soon found it was easier to develop her taste for Japanese food. Rugs went

46

down over the tatami, and these, with the use of wood stoves, helped to take the chill off the house, but it was never really warm.

She had been in Morioka for a year when Kuni Obara returned from the United States. Kuni was now unusually well qualified to teach in Japan where a graduate degree from an American university was regarded with great respect. Tommy had insisted that there be no strings attached to Kuni's education; she was free to make her own decision as to her future life work. As soon as she landed, Kuni began to receive attractive offers from schools seeking trained Christian teachers, but she turned them down. "I felt that I wanted to spend my life where it would count for more, and where other people were not willing to go. So I joined forces with Miss Allen and went to Morioka."

Once settled in Morioka, Tommy found herself busy with three different types of work: She supervised the Uchimaru Kindergarten and worked closely with the kindergarten Mothers Club, she had overall supervision for women's and children's work in the Morioka Field, and she established and directed the Shinjo Center — the community center of which she had dreamed and for which she had long planned.

The Uchimaru Kindergarten was the oldest Baptist kindergarten in the north and one of the earliest Christian kindergartens in Japan. As early as 1907, Mrs. Eiko Nagaoka, a teacher in the Morioka High School, read about work being done with preschool children in Europe and the United States, and she appealed to the local Women's Christian Temperance Union to begin a kindergarten. There were few women in Japan who had been trained for such work, but one of them, Mrs. Henry Topping, was a Baptist missionary in Morioka. She agreed to begin a school for preschool children. The Baptists owned an old house which had been the mansion of a feudal lord one hundred and fifty years before, and this became the new school. While the building was being renovated, the carpenter who was cutting windows in the gloomy old walls remarked, to the delight of the missionaries, "They want us to make this a house of light."

Tommy's second responsibility was for the women and children of the Baptist churches in the Morioka field. At scattered

towns throughout the northeast there were several small, struggling churches. She became familiar with their names, Hanamaki,
Kamaishi, Taira, Tono, Hachinohe, and Kesennuma, and she also
became familiar with their problems: This one had no pastor,
but the members were conducting the services; that one had lost
the church building in a fire, but the members were meeting in
homes; one needed to open a kindergarten; in another the
women's group was made up entirely of older women and offered
nothing to young mothers. Her reports carried honest words
about the churches in the north. Ofttimes the reports were discouraging: "The church here is probably less adequately
equipped to meet its opportunity than any in northern Japan."
Sometimes the reports were encouraging: "From an organization
that had to be practically carried, they have grown into a group
that makes and carries out its own plans."

The Shinjo Center stood at the edge of town where the
farmer's rice paddy mingled with the shop of the fishmonger and
the cottage of the craftsman. Neither city nor country, the area
was well beyond the reach of established churches and kindergartens. Here Tommy and Kuni conducted a variety of activities
in the best tradition of a neighborhood house. Boys' and girls'
clubs met at the center, working girls came there for night
classes in English and Bible, and each week there was Sunday
school. Young girls from the country came to live at the Center
and learned how to teach kindergarteners in their own villages.

During summer vacations Tommy tried out some of her own
ideas concerning community evangelism. She began a series of
children's summer schools in the small towns of the area where
there was no Christian witness. "It's not exactly fair to call it a
Daily Vacation Bible School, I guess, when they didn't know
anything about the Bible." With six or seven workers Tommy
stayed in each village for a week or ten days, usually living in
the public school. Each day four or five hundred children came
to the school.

Matsuo Kozan was a mining town in the mountains where
some three thousand people lived, and the men worked in the
nearby sulphur mines. To reach Matsuo Kozan the summer
school workers left the train at the foot of the mountain and

picked their way along foot trails for two hours before they reached the top. Here they found a singularly cheerless community where no trees grew and no flowers bloomed; the plants could not face the sulphur fumes. But they did find a warm welcome from children, teachers, and parents.

Doors of all kinds were open to us, so that it was not just a vacation school for children, but it reached out and touched all of the community. Two afternoons a week I conducted cooking classes for the women. That sounds big, and those who know my limitations will doubtless be overcome with mirth or surprise, or both! Some of the women had asked beforehand if I would teach them some foreign cooking, and I became proficient in fixing rice cakes, omelets, and Spanish rice, teaching about eight or nine dishes in all. Even though I may be accused of boasting, I will say that it was a huge success.

Every night we had meetings for the young men, conducted by Mr. Imai, the Morioka pastor, preceded by an hour of hymn practice. They never seemed to tire of singing! The young women asked if they, too, might have a chance to learn some hymns, so two nights were given to them for hymns and a talk. When I asked if they would like to play some games, they clapped their hands in glee just like children, for there was so little joy or color in their lives.

It was during the year 1931 that Christmas came in July. The theme for the children's school was Love, and the motto was John 3:16. Each day there were stories of the love of parents, the love of others, the love of nature, and the love of God. There were five classes with an average of sixty children to each class, and each class prepared one of the scenes of the Christmas pageant. Excitement mounted as the children made a gold paper crown for Herod and turned Japanese carrying cloths into Palestinian headdresses. When the big night came, all the citizens of Matsuo Kozan were on hand for their first Christmas pageant.

After the pageant came the party. Producing Christmas decorations for the party in July on top of a sulphur mountain in Japan was a challenge. An old Christmas card from America provided pictures of camels and wisemen which were mimeographed on sheets of paper and then made up into bags for candy. The mountain children knew few of the sweets that children in the cities enjoyed, and they found the Christmas bags of candy a rare treat. Tommy was touched when, at the end of the evening, the adults stayed to clean the stage, to pack away the costumes, and to clean and scrub the floors.

Thus Christmas came to the children of a sulphur mining town on a barren mountaintop in backwoods Japan, and with it came a little bit of reverence and awe and a little of joy and love. "When we left at the week's end, the children accompanied us down to the road. We felt as Paul must have felt when the people came to see him off."

Each summer, from 1929 to 1937, Tommy and the other workers went to villages where there was no Christian work and held schools for the children. Those were the years of the war in China, when Japan's relations with the United States were deteriorating, and foreigners often met with suspicion and hostility from the Japanese people. Tommy and the other workers found they could go on, and that parents and village officials were grateful for the training their children received.

 It was this program that caught the attention of the Re-Thinking Missions group. They were so intent upon Christianity not being just an ivory tower and not being confined within the walls of the church. They thought that Christians should get out among those who know nothing at all, to sow the seeds and to try to follow up results.

The summer school program had indeed caught the attention of the Laymen's Missionary Inquiry. Dr. Charles P. Emerson, Dean of the Medical School of the University of Indiana, one of the members of the committee, wrote to Tommy, "Please don't think that I am flattering you, but I do want to tell you that in our commission you stood out as one of the three or four missionaries in the Orient whose work thoroughly appealed to us."

The Laymen's Missionary Inquiry was an effort to survey and evaluate the effect of one hundred years of Protestant missions in Asia. It was sponsored and financed by the laymen of the Presbyterian, Dutch Reformed, United Presbyterian, Methodist Episcopal, Congregational, Protestant Episcopal and American Baptist churches.

Mature thinkers realized that there were difficulties in the foreign mission movement which had not been foreseen in its early days. The destruction of Oriental spiritual values by the inroads of western culture had left thousands of Asians rootless. Although closely connected with the introduction of western culture in general, Christianity seldom kept pace with the impact of technical, industrial, and economic thought. The introduction of non-Christian western ideologies further confused the compound. The result was often a renaissance of eastern religion as national leaders recognized the danger of a lack of ideological focus in national life or the denial of any religious belief and the adoption of a completely secular philosophy. Against this background a comprehensive study of the Asian mission fields was undertaken by a committee of fifteen prominent laymen under the chairmanship of Dr. William E. Hocking, Professor of Philosophy at Harvard University. In 1932 they published the results of their work in the book, *Re-Thinking Missions.*

One of the points stressed was the necessity of recognizing the values in other religions and seeking points of contact with them. Christianity should, the authors stated, avoid polemics and claims of exclusiveness. It would be better to join with other religious men in a search for greater and wider knowledge of religious truth than to assert the uniqueness of Christianity, they said.

The argument which arose following publication of the book was part of a larger theological dispute which was already a feature of contemporary religious life. Professor Hendrik Kraemer, Dutch professor of religion, took issue with the results of the Laymen's Inquiry in a report prepared for the Madras Conference of the International Missionary Council in 1938. It was his view that the Christian message is a unique revelation designed to displace rather than to supplement other religions. But Dr. Kraemer also pointed out that the theological issues raised by the commission report had unfortunately obscured the very valuable practical suggestions that it contained.

As commission members looked at the churches of Asia, they saw groups which tended to withdraw from Asian society. Foreign ecclesiastical forms, missionary domination, and the use of an alien tongue helped to set the Christian apart from his neighbor. They deplored the lack of rural participation in the church in Japan and urgently recommended that agricultural missions be organized. No mission board, noted the laymen, had ever sent an agricultural missionary to Japan. Missionary evangelists had been assigned to country work and had succeeded in establishing churches in a few small towns and villages. But too often missionary effort was thinly spread, and there was too little trained leadership among national Christians to follow up the itinerant work of the missionary. Besides, there was little money for the country, for mission funds were usually committed to maintaining urban work, and there was little to spare for rural evangelism.

Dr. Kenyon Butterfield, President of Massachusetts State Agricultural College and vice-president of the American Board of Commissioners for Foreign Missions, was the leading American proponent of agricultural missions. As early as 1928 he had presented a paper at the meeting of the International Missionary Council at Jerusalem, summarizing his concept of an effective plan of rural improvement. The farmer's lot could not be bettered, he declared, by anything short of a comprehensive plan that included social, educational, medical, and economic changes. He believed that only by showing a concern for the man, the family, and the community could Christianity substantially penetrate rural Asia.

In 1931 Dr. Butterfield was sent to Japan under the auspices of the International Missionary Council. After studying the peculiar problems of rural evangelism in Japan, he met with Japanese churchmen and missionaries to consider the ineffectiveness of previous efforts and the lack of a philosophy of rural advance. Dr. Butterfield recommended a plan of comprehensive evangelism which called for centrally-located rural churches ministering to surrounding towns. He also stressed the need for dedicated, well-trained Christian workers who were willing to live in the country and to become part of the community.

One Japanese churchman who was always alert to the needs of groups beyond the reach of the Christian church was Dr. Toyohiko Kagawa. The Kingdom of God Movement launched by Dr. Kagawa in the late 1920's was an effort to evangelize the farmers and the industrial workers. Backed by the International Missionary Council and supported by the Japanese churches, it absorbed the energies of the Christian community for several years, but the results were disappointing. Dr. Kagawa, too, saw the need for a different approach in the country.

Tommy was, of course, aware of the studies and the discussions going on in Japan and elsewhere. Fifteen years of practical experience in Japan, most of it far from the urban centers, plus her own contacts with farmers, their wives, and their children, suggested to her the weaknesses of the methods of the past and the need for a new approach. She continued to visit the churches in the Morioka field and to help in their women's meetings and in their kindergartens, but she was beginning to wonder if the consuming concern she felt for the country people might not be a call to a field of further service.

Chapter Seven

AT THE END OF THE ROAD WAS KUJI

ONE DAY IN 1930, while Tommy was attending a meeting of the graduates of the Uchimaru Kindergarten, she met young Takeshi Yahaba. He was a Morioka boy who had been attending college in Tokyo, but he was then at home recuperating from a three-year bout with tuberculosis. Several days later she bumped into him as she hurried down the street. They talked together for a few minutes, and on an impulse Tommy asked him if he would come to the Shinjo Center and help with the boys' club. He said that he didn't know anything about boys' clubs, but he promised to come if he were needed.

Takeshi was the second oldest son in a family of four boys. His grandparents owned what had once been a prosperous whole-sale and retail drug business, and his mother worked hard both in the office and the home. But his father paid little attention to the business or to his family, and Takeshi's childhood was one of turmoil and sorrow. He recalls:

> It was very hard for us four little boys; our father was drinking and away from home a great deal. We became financially hard up, and often there was not enough money to pay our school tui- tion. I began to feel desperately sorry for my mother, for she was always the first one up in the early hours of the morning and the last one to go to bed at night. I started making plans to become a businessman and to make money for the sake of my mother.

When he was small his mother enrolled him in the Uchimaru Kindergarten, but the family was Buddhist and regularly took the boys to the temple on memorial occasions. As he grew up,

54

his home was so unpleasant that he stayed away as much as he could and joined other boys in street gangs. One time he led a gang in throwing stones at a small Salvation Army house and ridiculing the Salvationists. His only consolation was his love of sports, for he could forget his troubles when he skated or played baseball. But most of all he loved running, and he was proud of the races he won at the school athletic meets.

His ambition to succeed in business became more intense as he grew older. By working a full eight-hour shift at the post office and peddling medicines from door to door on weekends, he managed to pay his high school tuition and to help his mother financially. Bitter questions filled his mind as he bent over his books or tramped through the windy streets selling medicine.

> I would look at other children's homes and see that they had a nice homelife in comparison with mine, and I wondered what made the difference. Why was my father that way? Why didn't we have enough to eat? Why had we lost all our money? I wondered why everything was so hard for us, and I kept asking — why, why, why?

When Takeshi graduated from high school, Japan was in the grip of a depression, and jobs were scarce. His business high school diploma meant little during such hard times, and the only job he could find was as a sweeper in a garage. There he found himself shocked by the low conversation and moral level of his fellow workmen. Even his own home life had not prepared him for the standards of the mechanics and drivers around him.

On his way home one night, tired and depressed by his companions and stained with the grease of his trade, his restless mind kept turning over schemes to make more money. Stopping in a bookstore, he picked up a New Testament and glanced through it. He paused to read the story of Zaccheus in the nineteenth chapter of the Gospel of Luke, and he recognized his kinship with the biblical businessman. "Oh," he said, "this tells about me exactly! I want money — my one aim in life is to get money and then more money!" That story of Zaccheus appealed to him. Zaccheus was changed by meeting Christ, but who was this Christ; what did he do; and how could he change a person's life like that? Could he change Takeshi's life too?

It took Takeshi a long time to answer his question. That same summer the baseball team from a Christian school, Rikkyo (St. Paul's) University, made a tour of Japan and played in Morioka. Takeshi, who had lost neither his love of sports nor his athletic ability, was thrilled by the appearance of the team. It seemed to him that if he could go to school and play on the Rikkyo baseball team, and at the same time learn something about Christ, he would fulfill his highest ambitions.

Although there had been some improvement in the family fortunes, Takeshi's decision to attend Rikkyo touched off a stormy scene. His father and his older brother flatly refused to allow him to attend a Christian school. But the second Yahaba son had a very strong mind! He was stubborn, and, when he made up his mind, he wasn't going to change it. He had decided to go to Tokyo, and to Tokyo he would go. His father finally gave in and said he would send him ten yen a month for food. So off the young man went.

Takeshi was well-received at Rikkyo. His teachers were impressed by his story and by his manner, and they arranged for him to receive financial help from Bishop Norman Binsted, Bishop of Iwate Prefecture. Takeshi settled down to study, and he also began training for the coming Olympic trials. The 1936 Olympics were to be held in Berlin, and hundreds of Japanese athletes were working to fit themselves for international competition. Each month Takeshi clipped a few seconds from his time, and he knew that he had an excellent chance of joining the Olympic track team.

Working, studying, and running, Takeshi was busy and happy until he caught a bad cold. He had brought medicines for almost any illness from home, and he took the cold remedies that he had on hand. But this cold was different; the medicine didn't seem to help, he was tired and feverish, and he was steadily losing weight. At last he went to St. Luke's hospital for diagnosis, and after an examination the doctor broke the news that he had developed tuberculosis. He had, at best, only three months to live. Shocked and stunned, Takeshi started for the door and fainted, and only after five hours of treatment was he able to return to his room.

Three months to live! There was nothing to do but to go back to his home in Morioka. Things were in a tragic condition there, for his erring father was seriously ill, and his mother was struggling to care for him as she worked to earn the necessities of life. There was nothing for Takeshi to do but to lie on his mat and think about the fact that he was going to die.

The disease continued running its relentless course. Takeshi's fever climbed higher and higher, and he became weaker and weaker. His brother brought a doctor to see him, but there was little the doctor could do. His mother turned to traditional remedies, bringing little pellets of paper that had been blessed by the gods in the nearby shrines and temples. Recognizing that his mother was trying desperately to help him, Takeshi dutifully swallowed the pellets, reasoning that if he were going to die anyway, they could do no harm. Then his mother called in a practitioner of moxa. This woman heated a mulberry stick to a white heat, covered it with a newspaper, and touched the stick to four spots on Takeshi's chest. Moxa proved no more effective in curing tuberculosis than the paper pellets from the shrine gods.

Once he had recovered from the original shock of finding himself seriously ill and facing death, Takeshi's will to live came back to him despite the failure of the various treatments. He had unanswered questions, and he did not intend to die until at least some of them were answered. He realized that his cure would depend on his own efforts. Patiently he rested in the sun, slowly he began to exercise, and at last he could walk again.

> I was sick from beginning to end exactly three years, and during that time I didn't read anything but the Bible. Still I was not satisfied; I wanted to find out more about this wonderful book.

The death of his father left the family in debt, and as soon as Takeshi was strong enough, he went to work. He obtained a position in a department store to help out during the busy season preceding New Year's, and soon one of the executives offered him a permanent position. Since he liked the business and he needed the money, it seemed as though this was his great opportunity to assure the financial success he had always desired.

But by this time Takeshi had met Tommy, and his questioning mind was at work again. As he showed the boys at the Shinjo

Center how to use a jigsaw to make trays and bookcases, or coached his pint-sized baseball players, he wondered why Tommy and Kuni cared about them, and, indeed, why he cared about them, too. Sunday school work and the telling of Bible stories were a challenge to him.

His final year in Morioka was a year of spiritual struggle for Takeshi. His family, his friends, his teachers, and his business associates urged him to continue in merchandising, and the money in his pay envelope was very real to him. Yet, he had begun to look at the country around him in a new way, and he began to wonder if this growing awareness might be a call to Christian work. New questions arose during one of the famine years that periodically occur in northern Japan.

> I saw Kuni-chan and Miss Allen gathering relief goods and taking them to different villages, and I wondered why other people weren't helping with this service. Why did the missionaries do it? It was hard work. Why did they have to do it alone? What motivated them, and why didn't that same feeling motivate others? Why wasn't there a man to help them?

Takeshi was not the first Christian to see the need for a man to do something and then to suspect that he was that man. He turned his back on the glittering promise of the cash register and elected a life of service. To prepare for this life, he made his way back to Tokyo and to Rikkyo University.

Tommy had a close friend, Miss Lena Daugherty, a missionary of the Presbyterian Church in the United States of America who was in charge of a small settlement house in the Fukagawa slums of Tokyo. Arrangements were made for Takeshi to live at the settlement house and help with the work while he was going to school. There was a small salary, barely enough for him to buy his food; but his neighbors were laborers, and they taught him how to live on the few yen he had to spend.

As Takeshi progressed in his studies, he began to question the episcopal form of church government and to wonder whether he could work under the direction of a bishop. He talked often with his professors as he tried to work out the problem of ecclesiastical authority for himself.

At last he decided that he would have to have freedom to

make his own decisions, and that he probably could not work productively under episcopal direction. With the bishop's blessing, he left the Episcopal Church and was baptized as a Baptist in a Tokyo church. Tommy and Bishop Norman Binsted were close friends; they had been fellow passengers aboard the *Mongolia* in 1915, and they shared a common concern for the people of the north. The question of proselytizing did not arise between them, so when Takeshi returned the tuition money which he had received, the Bishop accepted it reluctantly. But Takeshi insisted that it was money provided by Episcopalians to train men to serve the Episcopal Church, and he had no right to its use.

The final influence, and an important one, in the forging of Takeshi Yahaba, rural evangelist, was Merrell Vories. During one of his college vacations Tommy sent Takeshi down to Omi-Hachiman near Kyoto to meet Mr. Vories and the members of the Omi Brotherhood.

In the 1930's, thoughtful, disturbed Christians such as Dr. Kenyon Butterfield and Dr. Toyohiko Kagawa had endorsed a technique for ministering to rural areas which came to be known as comprehensive evangelism. The basic idea lay in the belief that the Christian evangelist could be effective in rural Japan only by living with the villagers, participating in their daily life, and demonstrating Christianity rather than preaching it. Merrell Vories had pioneered in comprehensive evangelism even before the technique had been dignified by a name.

The founder of the Omi Mission hoped to confine his witness to areas beyond the reach of organized churches and to cooperate with them in every way. Such converts as the mission might make were to organize into denominations of their own choice. He felt that unification of Japanese and foreign workers was essential, and that every effort must be made to enlist and train Japanese leaders and workers.

Mr. Vories believed that there was a place for the independent missionary in the foreign field, and he thought that the men of highest ability should be where the problems were the greatest and that the use of resources could best be determined in the field. Mission boards were certainly necessary for the general missionary enterprise, but in his opinion there was also a place for special and experimental work by independent missions controlled in the field.

Takeshi's visits to Omi-Hachiman became more frequent. Here, he felt, was a place where the teachings of the Bible had been brought into daily life. Mr. Vories, in turn, was impressed by Takeshi and suggested that he might be interested in working with the Omi Brotherhood. But Takeshi knew too well the need for Christian work in the north, and he felt that it would be better for him to return home. Mr. Vories agreed that this was best, and he offered his help and guidance for any future projects that might become possible. "I will stay in the south," he told Takeshi, "but you must return to the north and begin the work that is so much needed."

In 1931 the black horse of famine rode forth through the northland. Spring was late, and day after day farmers waited anxiously for the sun to thaw frozen rice paddies so that they could transplant the seedlings into their plots of land. But the temperature lingered in the low registers, and, even when the weather began to get warmer, fog drifted across the muddy paddy land and blanketed the tiny plants. Late in the summer when the shoots began to head, the short and stunted plants produced few grains, and the farmers knew that they would have little to show when threshing time came. In the vegetable gardens the plants were late in growing and maturing, and there were few long carrots or big, white radishes. The heads of cabbage were small, and the greens produced only a few small leaves. Then, almost before the crops had gotten a start, it was winter again, and the villagers knew that they faced hunger and privation. It was the worst famine in forty years, and Tommy set out with two Japanese friends to survey the famine area.

 I took a trip, walking all over Iwate Ken, but especially the very poor area along the seashore. There was no other way to get there, and we walked fifty miles over nothing but mountain paths where there were no roads. I'm positive that there was not one bit of level ground in the whole fifty miles — not an inch! I had never seen a mountain until I was grown, because I lived in Indiana where it was very flat, and for me to walk fifty miles over a highland path was really something. We came to one peak, the top of which seemed to reach to the heavens. We were told that it was called Mount Resignation because the prefectural officials had gotten that far and said, "We would rather resign than climb that mountain." I knew what they meant, and I understood their feelings; but we climbed that mountain, and many more.

After the little band of relief workers had covered the famine area and talked with the country officials to learn their real needs, Tommy went back to Morioka and wrote to a friend in Tokyo, asking her to contribute something toward the aid of these destitute people. The letter was published in the *Japan Advertiser* and soon money and relief goods began to pour into Morioka in care of Thomasine Allen.

 I was quite astonished, for I had no idea of doing all that! The next thing was to administer the supplies, and that was a big job. We tried to distribute the things as justly as possible. Sometimes it was better to give money and sometimes it was better to send food or clothes. All this took a great deal of time, but it gave us wonderful contacts with the people.

Administration usually meant that the administrators transported the goods on their own backs to the needy in the isolated villages.

 The people we met would say, "What are you selling?" I would reply, "Oh heavens, I'm selling nothing! I'm trying to give this away; it's heavy!"

In Tayama the school principal was the contact man. He told the relief team that Tayama had never had to ask for help before, but this year sixty-one of his pupils were in desperate need of food, and two hundred were in need of clothing. These little children came to school after a breakfast of broth with a little barley and a few finely-cut radish leaves. They had no lunch, and they went home to a supper of the same broth.

"Yet they come to school regularly," said the principal, "and it is all I can do to keep back the tears as I stand before them."

Before the food and clothing distribution he spoke to his ragged and hungry charges:

"We have never had to receive help before, but this year has been unusual in the failure of the rice crop. Up to now we have not received anything, and these ladies representing Christianity are the very first to relieve our need. You must not think that you can receive things or depend upon others all the time. This winter you cannot help it, but, as soon as spring comes, you must work hard in order to help yourself and others. And every morning you should thank God for his kindness to you."

Solemnly the urchin mountaineers bowed to the principal and to their visitors. Large dark eyes looming in pinched faces strayed to the bundles of clothing and the sacks of food.

As we stood looking down into their little pitiful, sallow, but earnest and attentive faces, knowing that they were oh, so hungry, the tears streamed down our cheeks. Then the principal lined them up, called out their names, and told us what to give, for he had looked up the needs of each home. The children came to us solemnly in their ragged kimonos, and with many bows received their little bundles of food and clothes. As I stood giving out the food, my feet, encased in several layers of wool, were so cold I could scarcely stand it. Although it was ten degrees below zero, I saw several barefoot children and others in ragged socks, and then I was heartily ashamed of myself for even thinking about my own feet.

The mayor of a district with three small villages wrote for help. This district was five miles from the nearest train station, and the snow was heavy when the relief workers arrived.

First we stopped to see an old man nearly blind with trachoma. He could see just enough to weave crude straw leggings which brought him an income of about five sen a day. On this he supported his little six-year-old orphaned granddaughter and himself. Their food was mostly barley and water, and he had no fire. Friends had brought him a little brushwood from the mountains, but he was saving that to cook his food and could not afford to have a fire to keep himself warm. His clothes were ragged, and he was barefooted, and of course there were no mats on the floor. He would put his hands against his body to warm them when they got too cold to work; and, if the cold was too terrible, he would climb into some straw. We left clothing for him and for the little girl, and later we made arrangements to supply them with fuel.

In another place we visited, we found four orphaned children living alone, the oldest of whom was a boy of fifteen. A short time before our visit the youngest, a child of four, was taken suddenly ill and died in the night. Without telling anyone, the other children got a box, put the body inside, and said a prayer to Jizo-San; and then the boy put the box on his back, took a spade, and together they quietly buried their little sister.

But relief work was not all snow, wind, and cold. There was sunshine, too, for the fortitude and bravery of the unfortunate and the privilege of taking them a bit of warmth and cheer was most rewarding. However, they, too, found ways to make their contribution.

One night we found ourselves in a tiny village too tired to walk another step, and we sought shelter in a farmer's hut. "Why," he said, "we do not even have lights, and our home is too poor. Please go on to the next village." We told him that we had candles with us, and we asked him to please just give us shelter. He guided us to his house and broke the news to his wife who labored with him in the open all day. She hastened to put down some mats on the floor and to fix a fire. Pine twigs burning in a kettle furnished the heat and about as much smoke as warmth. We lit our candles, one by one, and felt that we were in another generation as we all sat around the little fire and talked with our host and his family. Never had we been treated with greater hospitality and courtesy. They gave their best and we appreciated it to the utmost.

Before she slept the sleep of exhaustion, Tommy's mind drifted back to the folklore she knew so well, and she recalled the words of the disguised regent who had been royally entertained in humble circumstances.

 The glow of that fire remains in my heart to this day. At the end of that long mountain trip was Kuji. We had gone along the coast, through all of the coastal villages, and Kuji was the end. That summer we decided that we would have one of our vacation village Bible schools in Kuji, so my first contact here goes back to 1931.

Two years after that, in 1933, there was a terrible tidal wave that completely washed out several villages. Many lives were lost and much damage was done, so we started out on another relief trip, and we walked through many of the same places. One little village where we had slept one night during our first trip was completely wiped out, and there was nothing left but the school building; everything else was gone. We administered food as we walked on and on, helping the people and making wonderful contacts with the authorities in Iwate Prefecture. At the end of that trip, too, was Kuji.

Chapter Eight

WHERE THE NEED IS GREATEST

BACK IN MORIOKA AFTER HER RELIEF TRIPS Tommy found herself unable to forget the people who lived in the forests and fields and along the seacoasts of northeastern Japan. She could not forget the patience and courage of the women who worked long hours in the field and then dragged themselves home to tend to their families. She understood the hopelessness of the men who left their women to farm the unproductive soil and went away to work as laborers in lumber camps or seaports. But it was the memory of the children which was most vivid, the children who were cold and hungry, the children who came to school poorly clothed and shabby, the children who had so little chance for any spiritual training. She began to think about leaving Morioka where there were established churches and kindergartens and moving to a small town where there was no Christian witness at all.

Kuni Obara had tramped the country trails by Tommy's side, and she shared her vision and call. Kuni was willing to turn the work in Morioka over to other hands and embark on a pioneering venture in the country; but she had reservations. She wondered if Tommy, a product of an entirely different environment, could live with the Japanese as well as work with them. Kuni regarded Tommy as "experienced, yet inexperienced for this demanding work."

Takeshi Yahaba was still living and working at the slumside settlement house in Tokyo and doggedly pursuing his studies at Rikkyo University. During vacations he returned to Morioka to

64

help in the Shinjo Settlement House, to teach on Sundays, and to work in the summer vacation schools. He was fascinated with the new venture as he helped in the planning, and he volunteered to survey Iwate Ken and report on possible sites.

 I often told Mr. Yahaba, when he was starting out on those trips, "I hope you'll find that neediest place a little bit farther south because I'm tired of being cold all the time! The people in the south need saving just as much as those in the north." When he came back he asked, "Do you want to go where the need is greatest, or do you want to go where it's more comfortable?" Well, that kind of put me on the spot, and I replied, "Of course I want to go where the need is greatest."

Takeshi reported that the greatest needs existed in Iwate Prefecture, for there was no Christian work in the area — neither schools, nor social settlements, nor agricultural missions. And since the town of Kuji was the county seat, it seemed the best place to go.

Once this decision had been made, Tommy and Kuni submitted their request to the Japan Baptist Mission and were granted permission to transfer to Kuji. The problem of finances was a very real and a critical one. Tommy had her salary and working budget, and a friend had promised a gift of money for a building. But beyond these resources she knew that she could expect little from the Baptist boards except their blessing.

In the United States the American Baptist Foreign Mission Society and the Woman's American Baptist Foreign Mission Society were facing the worst crisis in their history. The country was in the grip of a severe economic depression, and its effect on the mission societies was disastrous. Each year the board members saw their resources cut away. Donations in 1935 were half of what they had been in 1931, and the income from invested funds dropped lower and lower.

When the board met in January, 1935, it faced a heart-breaking decision. "At the meeting . . . the Board came to realize that genuine disaster threatened the entire work unless resources were promptly, greatly, and permanently increased, or unless the work as a whole was readjusted to a narrower base." Since it seemed unlikely that they could expect any increase in either income or donations, the board decided to make a study of the entire foreign mission program and an evaluation of the "most, less, and least" essential projects.[3]

Two years later, in 1937, the committee reported that the ten fields in Asia and Africa "had been carefully and critically surveyed." The committee stated that a substantial saving could be effected only by abandoning major projects — "geographical areas, racial groups, important institutions, or entire fields." Therefore, it was the decision of the two societies that they would endeavor to maintain the existing work "to the degree that the denomination makes it possible."[4] The final resolution of the problem was to cut the appropriations for South India, Japan, and East, South, and West China by ten per cent and the appropriations for Burma, Bengal-Orissa, Assam, Congo, and the Philippine Islands by fifteen per cent.

Dr. William Axling, member of the Japan Baptist Mission, expressed the anguish of the missionaries in the field when he wrote to the American Baptist Board to protest the retrenchment. "This is tragic for those of us out here on the firing line. The battle against sin, secularism, materialism and the mechanistic interpretation of life and the universe grows apace, but the missionary personnel dwindles and cut follows cut in working funds."

Despite the obstacles and the lack of assurance of financial support, Tommy felt that work could be opened in Kuji. She prized the friendship of the government officials which she had gained during the famine years, and she felt that here was a chance which might not come again. The mothers in Kuji had been pleased when their children attended the summer vacation school, and they asked Tommy if she could open a kindergarten. An experienced Japanese teacher left her work in Taira and stayed in Kuji for a year on an experimental basis; the experiment was a success. The town agreed that the children had benefited from their kindergarten work, and the mayor expressed his opinion that his people needed leadership training.

Tommy, Kuni Obara, and her sister, Kimi Obara, made the

[3] American Baptist Foreign Mission Society 1935 Annual Report, p. 17.
[4] *Ibid.*, 1937 Annual Report, pp. 21-23.

move to Kuji in 1938. They rented a house which the towns-people believed to be haunted, and each morning for days the neighbors hopefully inquired whether the ghost had appeared in the night. The ghost presented no problem, but there were other difficulties of life in Kuji which they had to meet. A round, deep wooden bathtub which they had brought from Morioka proved to be too large to fit into the house and had to be temporarily installed in the yard. While one member of the household bathed, the other two held up quilts to provide a measure of privacy. There was no water system in Kuji, and they had to carry all of their water either from the town pumps or from the river.

Much of the first year passed in simple, hard physical labor. Walls were scrubbed, drains were cleaned, and weeds were cut. Then March came with its promise of spring, and, even in the north, the hardy Japanese plum tree put forth its delicate blossoms. Kuni suggested that they celebrate the traditional Doll Festival on Girls' Day, March third. Five shelves were arranged as steps and covered with bright red cloth. At the top stood the Emperor and Empress dolls with little gold screens placed as a background. On the next shelf were three court ladies dressed in ancient court robes, and below them were the court musicians all diligently performing on old-time instruments. Doll furniture and some American dolls — who seemed quite at home in their exotic setting — completed the display.

They planned to serve tea and little bags of candy decorated with pink cherry blossoms, and at midnight they were still past-ing tiny blossoms on the bags, an exasperating chore for western fingers. When Tommy woke up the next morning, she found the little bags were finished — Kuni had worked all night.

The Doll Festival was a complete success. Of course the kin-dergarten children came, as well as the Sunday school students and fifty of the neighborhood children. They were dazzled by the display of dolls, and they asked curious questions and en-joyed the candy in the gay little cherry blossom bags. In the afternoon, from two to six, the grown people of the neighborhood came, and it was the reaction of the women which touched Tommy and suddenly brought home to her the unbelievable pov-

erty of life in Kuji. It seemed so sad to find that these women
and girls had never known the joy of one of their own festivals.

   Several of the women said that it was the first time they had
ever seen the doll festival, and it was hard to believe! But they
had always lived in this backward district, and they had never
had such opportunity. People in cities could see the dolls in the
shop windows, but country people did not even have this
privilege.

The little kindergarten flourished, and a second kindergarten
was opened in Okame, a little town about five miles from Kuji.
Tommy visited it frequently.

   I rode my bicycle out there at least two or three times a week
and sometimes every day. Frequently the wind would be so
strong against me that I had to pump going downhill. Then
I'd think, "Maybe the wind will be at my back coming home,
and I can just sail along." But almost invariably the wind would
have switched, and I'd have almost as much trouble getting back
as I had had going!

Older children came to Sunday school in Kuji and in Okame,
and soon it was possible to begin Sunday school classes in other
towns. There were one hundred children in the Sunday school in
Yamaguchi, fifty children in Kokuji, and thirty children in Osanai.
And soon there were over five hundred children coming regularly
to the Sunday schools held near Kuji.

Mr. Temma Nobechi came to Kuji in June, 1940, to visit the
village schools around Kuji. He was a children's evangelist, a
writer, and a gifted story teller; but his health was frail, and
Tommy knew that she could not expect their guest to walk or
bicycle over the rough roads that connected the villages. Takeshi
tells how he finally solved the problem for her:

Our means of transportation for him was fearful and wonderful.
Mr. Nobechi could not ride a bicycle, so I attached a rear car onto
my bicycle, and he sat on a little chair in the car as I pulled it.
Miss Allen went along on her bicycle too, although some of the
distances were rather great for all of us!

As far the children were concerned, the tour was a tremendous success. Spellbound, they heard for the first time of
Noah and the flood, of Joseph and his coat of many colors, and
of David and Goliath. But even here it was almost impossible to

escape from the mood of belligerent nationalism which was now
gripping Japan; one of the newspapers reported on Mr. Nobechi's
visit and retold the David and Goliath story, representing Japan
as David and the United States as Goliath.

Tommy knew that they must have a decent building for the
kindergarten as soon as it could be built, and Takeshi Yahaba
recalls the conditions of the first kindergarten quite vividly:

> The kindergarten was housed in a terribly dark, dirty Japanese
> house. We had no toys or playthings; only a swing made of a
> piece of rope hung from the limb of a tree. We had no chairs
> either, but we were able to pick up some tangerine crates, and we
> brought them to use as stools. We did have snakes in the yard, but
> we finally killed most of them. Worse than anything else, however,
> was having to use this terribly dark, unsanitary room for the chil-
> dren.
>
> No one wanted to sell land to Christians, and, after days and
> days of walking and conferring and trying our best to find a place,
> we were about to give up. Then an old woman in the country at
> the edge of Kuji said, "Well, I've heard that Christianity is a pretty
> good religion. I don't know anything about it; but they are work-
> ing for God, and we believe in gods, so maybe it's the same. Any-
> way, I will let them have a part of this land." Other people heard
> about this and talked it over, and finally, seven people in all de-
> cided to let us have some ground, and we were able to buy an
> acre of land at the edge of Kuji.
>
> When we were going through all this hardship we couldn't help
> wondering if it were God's will for us to stay here. It just seemed
> as though everything was against us, and yet we had a firm feeling
> that it *was* His will, so we went on. I felt the responsibility keenly
> because I was the one who had urged Miss Allen to come up
> here, and many a night I spent in prayer over it. What was the
> best thing thing to do? What was His will for us in this place?

The acre of land was a barren strip with a queer shape; there
were odd corners and jogs where neighboring farmers continued
to cultivate tiny plots, but the Christians had the land they
needed. After Takeshi finished the tedious negotiations, he declared, "We will call this God's Acre, for God has given us this
piece of land." The weary group held a brief thanksgiving prayer
meeting and dedicated the land to God's service.

Their pleasure was short-lived. Plans for the building had been
drawn by Merrell Vories, and construction was about to begin

when Tommy was summoned to the police office. There she
learned that a company from Kobe was building a factory in
Kuji to extract ore from the iron-bearing mountain sand. Their
plans called for a railroad spur that would run through the acre
of land they had so recently acquired. The chief of police pointed
out that the land must be sold to the Kobe company.

 I told him that I didn't see how we could give up the land,
so he let me go home and then called in Takeshi. He thought
that surely a Japanese wouldn't hold out, even though an American might. Takeshi was down there for three hours talking
to the chief of police, and bravely he told the man, "We are
going to do a greater work for Japan than you or the government can possibly do." One didn't talk that way and get away
with it in 1938, but he did.

"Governments," said Takeshi, "are concerned only with tem-
poral and material values; Christianity is concerned with eternal
and spiritual values." Then he launched into a careful explanation of Christian beliefs, and the chief of police busily recorded
in his book such unfamiliar terms as "sacrifice," "atonement," and
"resurrection." At the close of the three-hour conference the
chief of police said, "You may keep your land as far as the police
are concerned; we can't do anything with people that have the
faith that you have."

Arriving home with his news of the reprieve, Takeshi was
jubilant; but he was human enough to be sick from the ordeal
he had faced. Although the first round for possession of the land
had been won, the pressure was only beginning, and he cautioned
Tommy that the company officials would try to deal with her.
"If anybody comes," he warned, "just talk about the weather!
Or don't say anything; let me do the talking." Takeshi was right.
Soon a stream of business and company officials came to call.
They appealed to community pride and to patriotism, and they
even offered other land in exchange, but again and again Takeshi
repeated, "God gave us this land here on the edge of Kuji, and
we are not going to give it up."

As the discussion dragged on, construction on the building
began, and surveyors started surveying the land for the railroad.
All of the Kuji people were wondering who was going to win, the
surveyors or the builders. Finally, after Takeshi had repeated one

more time, "We are not going to give it up," the surveyors put away their transits and departed to build their railroad elsewhere.

Carpenters came to the construction site, but none of them stayed more than a few days. Some found the intricacies of western building beyond them, and others disliked the strictness of the overseer from the Omi Architecture Department. Finally a man reported to Tommy, saying that he was willing to work on the building until it was finished. She looked at him wearily and said, "I don't believe you at all when you say that you are going to be with us to the end!" He nodded and replied, "I don't blame you at all for not trusting any of us, but, Sensei, I promise you that I will be with you to the end." He stayed to finish the Center building — and to build thirteen more buildings in later years.

Shortages constantly halted the work, for metal was scarce and nails unobtainable. Tommy borrowed nails from a missionary in Sendai, and they collected old nails and laboriously straightened them, but still there were not enough. She finally went to Shanghai and bought twenty kegs of nails, enough to finish the building.

At last all of the difficulties lay behind them. The building was completed, and the kindergarten opened in bright, clean, and airy quarters. Registration threatened to swamp the new facilities, for plans made for fifty children were expanded to include sixty children, and then it was necessary to establish a waiting list of others whose parents begged, "It is all right if my child does not have a chair. Please just let her come anyway." On opening day, in 1939, the building was thronged with the relatives, the friends, and the curious.

Other visitors were interested in the building and displayed an unexpected appreciation of its beauty. A young electrician, one of thirteen children, came one day to fix a switch. His family was so poor that his mother peddled fish from two baskets swung on a pole across her shoulders to help to feed and clothe the children. Several days later he came back to talk with Tommy. "After seeing this lovely building, I have decided we must fix up our house; it *is* important to have a nice place to live. I want my father to come and see your nice floors and all, and maybe we can have a better home." Tommy was satisfied that the plan "to have a building so beautiful that it would reflect the life of Jesus, and demonstrate God's love in the physical surroundings" had been achieved.

Bishop Norman Binsted thought so, too. The Bishop, whose friendship for Tommy and interest in Takeshi had never flagged, was one of their first visitors. After he had returned home, he wrote to Tommy of the impression the building had made on him:

> The plan and workmanship are excellent, and no one knows better than I, what it cost in thought, prayer, and physical energy to erect. Others may have given the money to make it possible, but you and Obara San have put something of your own lives into it. I think this is what I was conscious of more than anything else. Your love and devotion have been wrought into the building, and that is why it is so beautiful.
>
> Then too, in spite of the depressing atmosphere of the present days, it is most inspiring to see two people who refuse to have their vision destroyed, and who dare to attempt great things for Christ. You are both marching in the right direction, and you can be sure that, just ahead of you, the Christ goes forward leading you on to even greater adventures for Him and His Church. There will be those who will try to pull you back, but Christ is not among them. He is out there in those hovels and off in those villages among the hills preparing the way for you and Obara San. You have no need for discouragement or doubt.

Chapter Nine

PLEASE DO NOT WORRY

                                    Sumire Jo Gakuin, Denenchofu
                                    3419, 1 Chome Tamagawa,
                                    Setagaya Ku, Tokyo
                                    April 10, 1943

Mrs. W. W. Bartlett
226 Hamilton Avenue
Westerville, Ohio, U.S.A.

Dearest Home-folks:

So glad to receive your letter last fall. It was good of you to take the chance and write even tho the circumstances were against you. I am with many friends in this internment camp and we are nicely treated so please do not worry. Will you please notify the Board and all other friends of my safety and good health. Red Cross gifts helped to make Christmas and succeeding days happier. All thanks to them.

Cherry trees bursting into bloom giving promise of spring and perhaps an opportunity of seeing you ere so much longer.

                                    Lovingly,
                                    Thomasine Allen

Examined by U.S.A. 131

FOR TWO LONG YEARS Tommy's mother and her sister Marguerite had had no word from her. For two long years they had waited together for the letter which finally came in the summer of 1943.

Marguerite, now Mrs. W. W. Bartlett, had returned from Shanghai before the war, and her mother, who was in ill health, had joined her in Westerville. Now they knew that Tommy was alive and had received one of the letters that they had hope-

73

fully dispatched into the void that divided the two countries.

In 1941 Americans in Japan watched with growing uneasiness the tensions that were building up between the two nations, and they struggled with individual decisions as to whether to stay in Japan or to return home. Many expatriate Americans had deep ties in Japan which made the decision a real struggle.

Tommy faced the problem early in 1941. On Washington's Birthday she was in Tokyo and went to the Embassy for a gathering of American citizens. The State Department suggested to those present that it might be better for them to return to the United States.

It was a very sad day for all of us because we didn't know what to do. If our State Department thought we ought to come home, then perhaps we should. On the other hand, there were some who thought that they might be able to help ease relations if they stayed. We didn't know what would happen to us if war came: whether we would be interned, whether we would be free, or whether we could help the Japanese or not. Each person had to decide what he himself thought best. Many went home, especially those with families, but there were some of us single people who thought that perhaps it was our duty to stay. I do not know whether we were right or wrong, but we couldn't do any more than live up to the best light we had at the time.

Tommy was certainly aware that the atmosphere in Kuji was tense, although it was not so much one of hostility as of fear. Friends who had come to see the building and who sent their children to the kindergarten were now worried and afraid of the police. They no longer dared to bow and exchange friendly greetings. When Tommy realized that the police were shadowing her, she decided that maybe her presence was hindering the work and making it hard for Kuni and Takeshi, so she talked it over with Kuni.

"What do you think I ought to do? So many of the missionaries feel they ought to go home. Do you think I ought to leave?"

"Are you afraid to stay?"

"No, I'm not afraid for myself, only of what they might do to you people or to the work."

There was a short pause and then Kuni asked softly, "Don't you think that we could suffer for our religion as well as you?"

After that conversation Tommy said no more about going.

She was in Kuji on Pearl Harbor Day, and at five o'clock in the morning five policemen came for her. They told her that she was to be interned, and that she should get dressed and pack warm clothes; but they would not tell her where she was going, nor did they mention the war.

 I did manage to get a little breakfast, and while the policemen were out walking around the house, I thought I'd burn up a few papers that were on my desk. I was just putting the last one in the stove when a policeman came in and said, "Don't burn that; don't burn anything; you may need them." So I desisted, but I learned later that after I had been taken away, they went through my house with a fine tooth comb. Believing that I was a spy, they tried to find anything suspicious at all. But they found only the little piece of paper I had started to burn, and it happened to be a recipe for a one-egg cake!

I was taken to the police station immediately and told to wait there until train time. The chief of police was most kind, and he said to me, "We do not want to intern you, but these are orders from Tokyo, and we have no other choice. We do admire you; we admire the work you have been doing, and we want you to come back after the war." Then I knew that the war had started, but when I asked where it had started, he said that was a military secret which I wasn't to know.

Takeshi was not at Kuji when the war began. His younger brother, Kozo, was in the Army and was due to return to Japan after a long tour of duty in Manchuria. Takeshi had gone to Kobe to meet him. As soon as he heard the news, he telephoned Kuji and learned of Tommy's internment, so he left at once for Morioka to meet the train and accompany Tommy and her guard to the interment camp. She managed to give him 300 yen which had not been confiscated, and they both knew that this sudden turn of events had placed on his shoulders the responsibility for the Center at Kuji. After seeing Tommy to the camp, there was nothing he could do but return to Kuji and begin the struggle for survival.

Tommy joined a small group of foreigners at the home of Mr. and Mrs. Gilbert W. Schroer at 71 Osawa Kwara Koji, Morioka. Mr. Schroer was a missionary of the Evangelical and Reformed Church who had been in Japan since 1922, and he and his wife were the only Protestant missionaries in Morioka in 1941. Besides Tommy, the Schroers, and their two children, there were four French Canadian Dominican priests and six Belgian Dominican nuns. The internees were housed in a social center building which was next door to the mission residence, and Tommy found that the vicissitudes of prison life soon bound them together. "We were one big happy family, although happy may not be the adjective to put there; but we did have many good times in spite of our fears."

These fears were very real. Mr. Schroer was taken away at once and sent to prison. His family knew nothing of the charges against him, and the guards could tell them nothing; it was months before they saw him again. "We didn't know where he was, and I had no idea what they were going to do to me because my work had been almost exactly the same as his. I kept waiting for the knock on the door thinking I'd be taken to prison too, and I kept a bag packed for that purpose."

Mr. Schroer had written an article about the villages of Iwate Prefecture, a survey of the people, their work, and social customs; for this he was imprisoned for months and questioned by the police. His family and friends did not know where he was until the following June. So the threat of prison hung over them and the guards used it to guarantee their good behavior.

 The government fed us, and the meals were adequate, but there was nothing fancy. I think that we suffered the most from the cold, for the stove in our room wouldn't burn, and in the room where we ate there was no fire at all. We were supposed to speak only Japanese so the guards could understand, but by using some French, some English, and some Latin, we got around the guards.

Of course, the hardest thing was not knowing what was going to happen. The two children were nine and eleven, and they were about the best sports of all, even though they had no other children with whom to play, and no toys and no books. We weren't allowed outside at all unless we had permission to walk in the garden for an hour or so, but it was so cold and snowy that we stayed indoors. Physically, it wasn't bad; our biggest troubles were mental.

It was awfully hard for us to celebrate Christmas, but we did. We had the creche, we sang the hymns; Catholics and Protes-

tants together, we kept our Christmas, but I think it was one
of the hardest Christmases that I have ever had. Of course, I
kept thinking about Kuji, wondering what they were doing that
Christmas.

After Christmas the Belgian nuns asked Tommy if she would
teach them the Japanese language. They had learned some, but
they wanted to continue their studies; and she suggested that
they take the Bible as a textbook, if the priest didn't object.

The priest gave permission, so every day we studied from the
Japanese New Testament. We made a chart and an outline of
each book in the New Testament, and then we made a general
outline of the Old Testament. They were very happy doing it,
and they have often told me how much they appreciated the
notebooks which we made at that time. It helped me, of course,
and I think it was a good thing all the way around. I feel
very close to them, and whenever I go to Morioka, I always
try to go out to the convent to see them.

In March of 1942 the Belgian nuns were allowed to return
to their convent, and Tommy, Mrs. Schroer, the two children, and
the Dominican fathers were transferred to Sendai where they
remained until September. That year the Swedish liner, *Gripsholm*, made its first trip to evacuate interned civilians, and
Tommy had to face once more the decision as to whether she
should stay in Japan or return to the United States. She felt
that she ought to remain in Japan until the Japanese government
ordered repatriation.

I just didn't see my way clear to go on that first exchange
ship. Our board had said in the beginning that it was up to
us out here to decide; that they would stand by us if we stayed,
and they would stand by us if we left. Each one should determine for himself what was the best thing to do, and so I
didn't go on that first exchange ship.

Now there were only thirty-nine Protestant missionaries re-
maining in Japan, and of this group there were six American
Baptists. Mrs. H. W. Topping was eighty years of age and had
retired; Mr. James F. Gressitt was not interned and remained in
Tokyo until his death in 1945; and Dr. and Mrs. William Axling,
Miss Alice Bixby, and Tommy, were interned.

In Sendai Tommy and Miss Bixby were interned with thirty Roman Catholic priests.

 Since there were so few of us women, we tried to do as much as we could of the so-called women's work for everybody. I remember that I was doing the washing one time and had a good many of the white Dominican socks in my laundry. One of the priests came along and said, "Oh, Miss Allen, you're doing all this work and not getting any merit for it!" I tried to tell him that I was not doing it for merit as they saw it.

The fathers were allowed to say mass in the church next door, and Japanese Catholics could come for the early morning mass at five o'clock. The policemen seldom inspected at that hour, and one morning one of the priests called Tommy over to the church, telling her that she had a visitor. The visitor was Takeshi Yahaba, bringing a big basket of persimmons as well as news of Kuji. He had also come to tell Tommy that he and Kuni wished to be married and to ask for her permission. Six o'clock came all too soon, bringing their brief reunion to an end. Takeshi returned to Kuji, and he and Kuni were married shortly thereafter by their friend Temma Nobechi, the children's evangelist.

Deprived of much that they had known of material comfort, the internees discovered unexpected spiritual resources. Tommy found great help in attending the services the fathers were allowed to hold.

 Months later I was asked how I looked so well when we had suffered from insufficient and inadequate food, and my reply was that man did not live by bread alone. What should we have done without this food for the inner man?

Then too, there was comfort and sustenance in the "candles of kindness" that blazed in their dark world, and they found that there was an unquenchable light in the human spirit and that the darkness comprehended it not.

 There was a candle of kindness with most of our policemen. I remember that the chief of police in Kuji, after he told me that I would have to be interned, turned to the policeman who was to take me to Morioka and said, "Don't walk by Miss Allen on the street. Don't sit beside her on the train. Don't do anything to embarrass her."

One time in Sendai several girls came with flowers which they wanted to give us. They were girls from the Christian schools,

Miyagi and Shokei. They wanted to show us that they sympathized with us and that they loved us in spite of the war. The guard turned them away, but they came back several times. Finally, seeing that they couldn't get in, some of them came to a house near the one in which we were interned, and they spent one whole evening singing and playing the little organ that they had moved outdoors so we could hear it. I think that evening of music was one of the most touching things that happened during the whole time.

Another time a little note was found which read, "Do not be discouraged. We are becoming stronger Christians because you are there suffering for us." I don't know who wrote it, but it was meant for all of us.

In September, 1942, Tommy was again moved, this time to a large camp in Tokyo. Here she found many old friends, including Dr. and Mrs. William Axling, fellow members of the American Baptist Mission; and she learned that life outside the camps had not been easy.

 Many times I thought, "Oh, my, if I could just be out; how much I could do!" But now I know I couldn't. The police insisted that it was for our own protection that we were interned, and, while I couldn't think so in the beginning, I finally came to see that it was very true. If we had been out alone, as many people were, life would have been much, much harder.

Among the old friends Tommy found in the Tokyo internment camp at Sumire Girls School was Mrs. Paul Mayer. Dr. and Mrs. Mayer were not interned during the first year of the war, but lived in their home in Mejiro Ku much as they had lived before. Japanese friends braved the policeman at the gate of their compound to bring them food, and a Japanese neighbor with a bomb shelter offered them hospitality in case of air raids. But for Mrs. Mayer the tension of loyalty and friendship for the two warring nations was almost unbearable. "It was like having a chronic headache; if you turned to the right, one side ached, and if you turned to the left the other side started. When we were interned it was a great relief to us," she later said.

The last months of 1942 passed, and Christmas came again. The internees kept Christmas as best they could, and, as 1943 dawned, they prepared to face another year of captivity. In the camp they organized the work of preparing vegetables, chopping wood, cooking, cleaning, and doing the laundry. Books were passed around to be read and reread, and discussion and study groups were organized.

While the internees sliced vegetables, washed socks, and studied together, the Japanese Army overran southeast Asia, conquered the Philippine Islands, Singapore, and New Guinea, and secured a toehold in Alaska. The United States, recovering from the shock of Pearl Harbor, threw itself into the conflict and, with a determined stand at Midway Island, turned the tide of battle and began to recover the lost Pacific islands. But of all this the internees knew little or nothing.

Once again arrangements were made for the Swedish liner, *Gripsholm,* to sail to Goa, the Portuguese protectorate on the Indian coast, to effect an exchange of Japanese and Allied nationals. Tommy was still undecided as to whether or not she should leave Japan, but the kindness of one of the Japanese guards helped her to decide. He had traveled out into the country to buy a basket of vegetables which he brought back and divided among the 130 internees, saying "You're all getting so thin, and we have not much for you to eat. All Japanese people are troubled by the lack of food." So when the time for decision came, it seemed kinder to answer the roll call: "Evacuate."

Takeshi and Kuni were allowed to come to Tokyo to tell Tommy goodbye. The guard assured them that they could stay as long as they wished, and that no policeman would listen.

In September the internees journeyed to Yokohama and boarded the *Teia Maru.* With blinds drawn and lights dimmed, the ship slipped quietly out of Yokohama Harbor to pick up internees in other ports before proceeding to Goa. At each port the precautions were repeated; all of the repatriates were gathered in the dining room, and the blinds were drawn tightly as additional passengers came aboard. Shanghai, Naha, Manila, Singapore; at each port men and women who had been caught by the rapid advance of the Japanese forces in 1942 came aboard the ship. Missionaries, businessmen, construction workers, entertainers, teachers, sailors, newspapermen; the passenger list was a cross section of the best and the worst of prewar expatriate

Thomasine Allen,
Student Volunteer, 1911

In 1947, Tommy
returned to Japan

Kuni Yahaba, Junko, Tommy, and Takeshi

Kuji, "the place where nothing was known"

"The mothers of Kuji . . . asked Tommy if she could open a kindergarten."

"A school for Shige Chan"

"A farm for skeptics"

"A hospital for Mrs. Asanai"

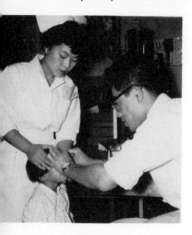 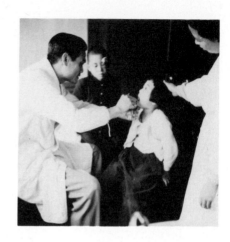

"A church for Mr. Osanai . . . the center and unifier of all our activities"

society. The *Teia Maru* was barely seaworthy, the food was poor, and water was rationed; but the passengers were on their way to freedom.

When they reached the Portuguese enclave, the *Gripsholm* was already in the harbor, and on October 19, 1943, the exchange was made. One by one the internees moved from ship to ship until 1,400 people had traded sides. The adults were restrained, but the children coming from Japan pounced like wolf cubs on the fruit, jam, and sandwiches which the sailors offered them. Of those coming from Japanese camps, 150 were critically ill, and fifteen were stretcher cases. Along with the stores necessary for her own voyage, the *Gripsholm* also carried Red Cross food and medical supplies which were transferred to the Japanese *Teia Maru* for shipment to American and British prisoners of war.

As the Japanese repatriates filed past, Tommy listened to their comments and noted their luggage with interest. At last she found the opportunity to whisper to them and to urge them to be careful in speaking of America and in displaying their American clothing and possessions. She warned them that there would be Japanese agents of the Thought Police aboard the ship, noting whatever they might say.

At last the formal exchange was over, and the repatriates abroad the *Gripsholm* found themselves in a world of fresh towels, plentiful supplies of soap, and ice water. There was plenty of water for bathing, there was a beauty parlor, and there were books, newspapers, and magazines. There was also a special Red Cross room with clothes and notions of all sorts, everything that the passengers might need. American movies had been provided by the American government. But best of all, there was food; none of the passengers ever forgot their first meal aboard the *Gripsholm*, a magnificent smorgasbord dinner.

Tommy joined a line for chocolate bars and moved forward step by agonizing step, only to have the supply depleted just before she reached the end. "I almost cried, I was so disappointed!" she recalls; but she was assured that there were more chocolate bars, and next day she was in the front of the line.

From Goa the *Gripsholm* set a course through the Indian

Ocean for Port Elizabeth on the Cape of Good Hope. Here the passengers disembarked for their first shore visit.

That was an experience I can never forget! The American officer lent us money to go shopping in Port Elizabeth; we could borrow fifteen dollars if we didn't have any money with us. When we disembarked, there was a whole big auditorium just filled with people waiting to welcome the "Mercy Ship" (that's what the *Gripsholm* was called), and they divided up so that everyone on our ship could be entertained in some home. The people from Port Elizabeth certainly were hospitable, and we could do anything we wanted to do during this short time that we were ashore.

Tommy found it almost unbelievable to have tea in a home with western furnishings. Here were chairs, tables, and tea poured from a silver teapot into cups of bone china. As she signed the guest book, she saw at the top of the page the name of a soldier whose home address was Indiana! Then suddenly she began to realize that she was free and back in the world she had known before.

From Port Elizabeth the *Gripsholm* sailed across the Atlantic bound for the port of Rio de Janeiro in Brazil. This was the second port call, and the passengers had another visit ashore.

An old friend of mine living there heard in some way that I was on the boat and came down to meet the ship. When he asked, "What is the very first thing you want to do?" I replied, "I want a chocolate ice cream soda." So we went to a very lovely place, and I had a wonderful chocolate ice cream soda. Then he asked, "What do you want to do next?" and I said, "I want to have a banana split." Before he got through with me, my friend thought that he probably would never fill me up.

It was now the middle of November, and the ship pulled out of the Rio de Janeiro harbor and headed for New York. The end of the long voyage was in prospect, and excitement aboard the *Gripsholm* mounted. "Since we all had hats that were terribly out of style, we planned that we would wave them to our friends, and then accidentally drop them in the ocean." But when the *Gripsholm* docked in New York, on December 1, it was under cover of darkness, and friends and relatives were not allowed to come to the pier. Instead, there were government officials and intelligence men to clear the passengers, and there were doctors and nurses to take charge of those who needed medical care. However, the reunion anticipated for so many years was not long delayed, for all of the friends and relatives of the passengers were waiting for them at the Prince George Hotel. "It really was a very, very remarkable evening, one that has to be imagined rather than explained," she later said.

Tommy's sister, Marguerite Bartlett, was among those waiting at the Prince George; but she was waiting alone, for on November 15 their mother, Lola Waggoner Allen, had died.

A reception was scheduled for all of the missionaries who had returned on the *Gripsholm*, and the general committee asked one person from each country to speak. Tommy was chosen to speak for those who had come back from Japan, and her sister watched proudly from the gallery of Marble Collegiate Church. Marguerite felt her mother's presence there in that great throng that had come to honor Tommy and the others who had returned on the *Gripsholm*.

Thin and physically exhausted, but strong in spirit and faith, Tommy rose to express what was in her heart.

 High on a mountain overlooking Rio there is a beautiful statue of Christ holding out His hands in loving invitation. As our ship sailed past this on our way to freedom, there was a lower hill that for a brief time blotted out the higher one; but soon the perspective changed, and we could see that in its true proportion, the hill which had loomed so large was really very small. But the statue on the montain was high and visible to the last, and the arms outstretched in the distance made it appear as a cross. "And I, if I be lifted up from the earth will draw all men unto me." May the time come when the lower hill of war will be passed and the cross on the mountain top be seen again as the outstretched arms of our Master invite both East and West, "Come unto me all ye that labor and are heavy laden; and I will give you rest."

Chapter Ten

THE PATRIOTIC HATCHET

INCIDENTS OF HYSTERICAL AND OFTEN SENSELESS violence had followed the shock of Pearl Harbor. In Washington, D. C., one courageous patriot, working in the dead of night, chopped down several of the Japanese cherry trees which surrounded the Tidal Basin and the Jefferson Memorial. Yukio Ozaki, donor of the trees, was one of Japan's great liberal statesmen and a former mayor of Tokyo. During the 1920's, in the face of growing jingoism, he encouraged the forces of democracy in the Empire, and he urged the maintenance of close ties with the United States. Mayor Ozaki nearly paid with his life for his democratic liberalism and his friendship with the United States. Assassins broke into his home during the murderous years of the 1930's, and only the cleverness of his daughter saved his life. By stalling the killers she gave her father time to escape from their patriotic swords. The unidentified American patriot also escaped from the Tidal Basin without detection but Mayor Ozaki's cherry trees lay dying in the midst of mud and snow.

Tommy had returned to a nation engaged in a colossal struggle for survival, to a nation fighting a two-front war which greatly strained its resources, and to a nation enduring many wartime restrictions. Yet, she found that freedom and justice were still very real and precious things in American life, and Tommy found it hard to become accustomed to such freedom again.

We had had to be careful for so long that I couldn't get used to the idea that once we were on the *Gripsholm*, we were really and truly free. I seem to have always considered myself a prisoner of war. Just before reaching New York, I told one of the officers that I would stay in New York for three weeks and then go on to Indiana. When he said, "Fine, but why do you think you have to tell me?" I replied, "Don't you have to report where I'm going and what I'm going to do?" He laughed and said, "Don't you know you'll be in America? You don't have to report to anyone." It was, in a way, my first feeling of what democracy is. I think that we Americans do not stop to think about democracy any more than we think of the water we drink; it's just a part of us. But after you've been confined for two years, and you suddenly become aware of one of the great principles such as freedom of speech, it really astonishes you!

Again, I was being entertained at a dinner in a restaurant, and the people were freely discussing the war and the coming of peace, when I cautioned, "Don't talk so loud. People at the next table can hear you." But my hosts responded, "Well, so what? This is America; we're free here, and we can talk!" And so I was astonished again. It was a long, long time before I really and truly *felt* liberated.

Late in December Tommy returned to Franklin to visit Mrs. M. E. Crowell and Mr. and Mrs. Robert A. Todd, friends of her childhood. *The Franklin Evening Star,* published by the Todds, had reported to its readers the progress of the *Gripsholm* as it neared the United States, and an interview Tommy had given in New York. "Which country do you consider home?" she was asked. "That's what the FBI asked me on the ship," she replied. "Of course I am an American."

Tommy began a two-year speaking tour at the First Baptist Church in Franklin. Under the auspices of the American Baptist Foreign Mission Society she crossed and recrossed the nation, speaking freely and frankly in churches in nearly every state.

The FBI knew what I was saying; they were on the job, all right, but they never interfered — not once. There were so few of us who had been interned in Japan during the war years that I felt it was my calling (if you want to put it that way), to talk about Japan and let people know firsthand what some of our experiences were.

At the beginning of my speech I nearly always said that everyone knew the dark side of Japan; they could see it in the newspapers, and they could hear it from other people. But there were only a few who could tell them of the better side of Japan during the war from their own experience. And so in all of my talks I never tried to minimize the bad parts; but I did try to emphasize the fact that there were kind people, even among the guards of the internment camps, and that there was a better side to the Japanese than what we saw in the papers. Many, many people used to thank me with tears in their eyes for telling them that there was another Japan. Of course, not everyone felt that way; many people came to the talks expecting to hear all about horrible atrocities. We were treated nicely in all of the camps in which I was interned, and I only told of my own experiences. We were hungry and cold most of the time, but as far as atrocities or anything like that, there were none. I'm sure that most of the church people were glad to know that there was this better side to Japan and to our internment.

When Tommy's speaking career came to an end in 1945, she decided that she would secure a position with the War Relocation Authority, the agency which administered the camps in which a large proportion of the Japanese-American population was confined during World War II. She felt that her background in Japan and her training in the Japanese language would enable her to serve both her own government and the internees.

Back of the decision to intern West Coast residents of Japanese descent in the United States, there was a long history of racial conflict. Many early American settlers in California shared a common Anglo-Saxon heritage, a high degree of patriotic pride, and an attitude of racial antipathy toward the Indians, the Latin Americans, and the Chinese whom they met in California. Chinese coolies, who worked in the mines and laid the railroad tracks, appeared to present a serious threat to the Californians, and, as time passed, the exclusion of Chinese immigration became a perennial issue in California politics. The battle was fought out in local and state politics and, finally, on the national scene. In 1882, when the United States Congress passed the Chinese Exclusion Act, the policy of the nation reflected the prejudice of the California miner and workingman.

The troubles between Californians and the Orientals in their midst did not end when the Chinese were excluded, for almost at once Japanese immigration began in significant numbers. The immigrating Japanese inherited the anti-Chinese prejudice, and political events in the Orient did nothing to allay the fears of the Californians. To many Americans the phrase, "The Yellow

Peril" began to seem something more than a jingoistic slogan. State politicans who had found political gold in the Chinese question found even richer veins in the Japanese question. Individuals and organizations mined the bonanza for all it was worth.

The United States government worked out an extra-legal arrangement with the Japanese government whereby Japan restricted emigration. This system was in effect from 1907 until 1924, at which time the United States Congress passed the Exclusion Act which bitterly offended the Japanese. A certain amount of prejudice lingered in the United States, but anti-Japanese agitation died down after the passage of the act.

On December 7, 1941, there were 127,000 persons of Japanese ancestry residing in the United States, and, of this group, 114,000 were concentrated in California, Washington, Oregon, and Arizona. Although regarded by their Caucasian neighbors as a tightly-knit community, the Japanese-Americans were actually divided into three distinct groups: Issei, Nisei, and Kibei. These were split into social, cultural, economic, and linguistic factions.

Issei were those Japanese who had been born in Japan. Although most of them were Japanese nationals, they were long-time American residents who had come to the United States prior to the passage of the Exclusion Act of 1924. *Nisei* were the sons and daughters of the Issei who had been born and educated entirely in the United States. Products of the American public school system, they were familiar with American ideals and political democracy, and they were primarily English-speaking. *Kibei* were also the American-born children of the Issei immigrants and citizens of the United States, but they had received all or part of their education in Japan. Those who returned to the United States were culturally and linguistically disadvantaged, and in the family group they were at odds with their Nisei brothers and sisters and with their parents who remembered a different Japan.

The attack of the Japanese navy upon American fleet bases at Pearl Harbor started a chain of events for the 127,000 residents of Japanese ancestry which had far-reaching repercussions. Shocked and frightened by the success of the initial attack and the wave of Japanese victories which followed, the American public was aroused to take severe action against the total Japanese group. It was decided that all residents of Japanese ancestry must leave the Western Defense Zone. Initially there were plans for resettling them in inland western states, but many states, caught in the hysteria of the times, refused to accept them.

For the evacuees it was a time of financial loss, heartbreak, confusion, and suffering. They were uprooted from their homes, ordered to dispose of houses, businesses, and automobiles, and shipped off to half-finished camps. On the whole, the evacuees behaved in an exemplary and patriotic manner, seeking to follow the often conflicting orders and patiently making the best of the situation. When the first director of the War Relocation Authority, Dr. Milton Eisenhower, left the Authority, he told the House Subcommittee on Finance, "I just cannot say things too favorable about the way they have cooperated under the most adverse circumstances."[5]

When Tommy went to work for the War Relocation Center, she was sent to bleak and isolated Tule Lake, California. Except for a few stubbles of desert grass there was no vegetation, and the slightest breeze raised clouds of sand and dust. The black tarpaper-covered buildings were utilitarian army barracks known as "theater of operations construction." Besides the housing areas, the administrative offices, and the military police barracks there were canteens for food, dry goods, shoe repair, and other essential services. Schools from kindergarten through high school were available for the camp children, and there were hospital facilities; but there was no doubt as to the prison atmosphere which prevailed, for barbed-wire fencing enclosed the camp.

When Tommy arrived at Tule Lake, most of the evacuees had been released, and the other camps had been closed. Tule Lake contained the disloyal Japanese, the hard core nationalists; or at least this was true on paper. In 1943 the government had screened the residents of all camps for loyalty using two questionnaires, one from the War Relocation Authority and one from Selective Service. The government planned to release all those

[5] Dorothy S. Thomas, Richard Nichimoto and others, *The Spoilage.* Berkeley: University of California Press, 1946, p. 38. (Before the Committee on Finance, May 15, 1942.)

whose answers indicated loyalty to the United States and to segregate in one camp those who were loyal to Japan. The plan looked simple on paper, but in practice it did not work out quite so neatly. The evacuees did not answer on ideological grounds. Some were afraid to leave the camp, fearing the discrimination, hostility, and hardship they would face on the outside; others based their answers on family loyalty, and all of them were suffering from a general disorientation which was the result of two years of confinement. In short, the questionnaires were a far from infallible way of determining national loyalty, for the residents of Tule Lake included Japanese nationalists who expected Japan to win and wanted to return to Japan. But it also included contented old men who saw no reason to exchange security for uncertainty, as well as others who simply wanted to wait and see what would happen.

In July, 1944, the Congress of the United States passed the Denationalization Bill which permitted Japanese who were citizens of United States to renounce their American citizenship. Hearings were held at Tule Lake from January 11, 1945, to March 17, 1945, and nearly six thousand applicants gave up American citizenship. But, in August, 1945, the war ended with victory for the American arms, and many Japanese who had renounced their citizenship now wished to regain it. Patiently the government began another series of hearings to determine which individuals might regain United States citizenship. Tommy worked closely with the camp authorities during these hearings, trying to interpret culture as well as languages.

 Many of the young Japanese rebelled at the way they had been treated by some of the authorities and at the fact that, although they were American citizens, they were interned. There were many diehards among the older Japanese people, and, of course, they influenced these rebellious young folk. Those who had been educated in Japan did not speak English, of course. It took a great deal of conferring with the Department of Justice, and I was able to be of some help, I felt, in explaining the American viewpoint to the Japanese and the Japanese viewpoint to the Americans.

Shortly after her arrival Tommy discovered that the camp residents were extremely curious about conditions in wartime

Japan. She was invited to speak to the Buddhist organization and talked for at least two hours as her audience listened with rapt attention and then plied her with questions.

 I explained that the living conditions of camps in America were palatial compared to what we had had in Japan. They had plenty of good food to eat, heat in their homes, and schools for their children. There was even a movie theater! Through the camp post office they could send and receive mail from the outside, but we in Japan had been allowed to write only one letter in two years. The freedom that they had in going about more than impressed me. But, of course, America was a different country and a richer country, so, in a way, they should not be compared.

Religious services at Tule Lake were held in a union church served by a Japanese-speaking pastor and an English-speaking assistant. Tommy was interested in noting the reactions of American Christians toward the evacuees. The American Friends sent layettes to the camp hospital so that each baby born at Tule Lake received a layette with his or her name on it, and at Christmas churches from all the states in the union sent enough Christmas gifts to the camp for all of the 18,000 internees.

One young Japanese postal clerk asked Tommy why the layettes were sent to the babies, adding, "I just can't understand this!"

"No," answered Tommy, "no, you can't understand it without a Christian background. You see, there was kindness in their hearts; they wanted to do something to show the love of Christ, and this was the one thing they could do."

Before long the postal clerk came back with several friends, saying that he wanted to learn more about this sort of thinking, and he asked Tommy if she would teach a Bible class.

 I was impressed by the Christian background in America which makes all the difference in the world. Again, we don't appreciate that blessing until it is taken away from us and we don't have it. It is something to make one pause and be thankful that he has been raised in a Christian democracy.

Chapter Eleven

THE YAHABAS ARE ALL WELL

FOR THREE YEARS TOMMY HAD NO WORD FROM KUJI. Then in 1946 she received a letter from Father Lamarr, a French Canadian Dominican priest and friend of her internment days:

> I could not find a Baptist chaplain, so I took a Catholic chaplain and we went up to Kuji. We took them some food. They welcomed us with open arms, and I was so glad to be able to see just how they were getting along. The town had been burned, not bombed, just burned; but your buildings are safe and they are being used. The Yahabas are all well. I have told them that they can write me, and I will forward the letter to you.

Soon Tommy received the promised letter and learned for the first time that a daughter, Junko, had been born to the Yahabas in 1944. "It was rather an overwhelming gladness that came to me," she said.

When Tommy was able to communicate directly with the Yahabas, she began to learn something of their experiences during the war. The first thing which Tommy learned was that some Japanese Christians had stood by them and had given them support from their own resources, but others had not.

Almost as soon as the war began, the Yahabas had begun to feel the opposition of the town, and the kindergarten enrollment began to decline as hatred and fear spread through the area and rumor was added to rumor. "Miss Allen was a spy," declared the rumor mongers. "The green tiles of her roof were a signal for the American Air Force." "In fact," they added, "she has been shot in Tokyo as a spy."

91

When the Yahabas could not buy their rice rations for lack of money, the villagers knowingly agreed that they must be receiving food from America. In desperation Takeshi watched their meager resources dwindle to the vanishing point. At first they had only twelve yen a month for food; then, as frightened mothers withdrew their children from the kindergarten, ten yen, eight yen, and at last, only five yen a month as income.

One night Takeshi sat with the three Obara sisters around the *kotatsu*, a covered fire pit used in the winter, and faced the fact that there was nothing at all in the house to eat. Not a grain of rice, not a vegetable, not a single potato remained. He had known hard times and hunger, but never before had he faced actual starvation, not only for himself but for those whom he loved. They went over the possibilities again and again. It was winter, and no vegetables could be grown until spring. The kindergarten enrollment would not increase, and they would be fortunate if the five children who were still attending would continue to pay their tuition. The bitter winds of Kuji rattled the shutters and scattered dust on the straw mats as they were forced to face the fact that there was no food and almost no money.

Then there was a sound at the door; was it the wind again? No, it was the sound of the door sliding open and the voice of the mailman, calling "Kawase!" Takeshi hurried to the entryway and found an envelope; inside there was a money order for five yen from Mr. Nobechi. Again and again the kind evangelist collected three or four yen from Japanese Christians, and he sent the money to his hard-pressed friends.

Takeshi's younger brother, Kozo Yahaba, was in the Army, and he, too, sent money from his meager soldier's pay when he could.

Then one day a telegram came which said, "Come to Tokyo immediately." It was signed by Mr. Shokuma Matsukata, and Takeshi lost no time in complying with the telegraphed summons. He put on his best suit, and, for the first time in years, a necktie. "I don't want to disgrace the country," he said.

The Matsukata family was one of the notable families of Japan, for, in the Meiji Era, Prince Masayoshi Matsukata was one of the advisers to the Meiji Emperor. He served his country twice as prime minister, and in his role of financial expert was credited with placing the Japanese Empire on a sound financial basis. The Matsukatas were members of a small group of Christian Scientists in Toyko, and during the year of the famine in 1931 and the tidal wave in 1933, this group and the Matsukatas had contributed generously to relief work in the north. Tommy had called on the family in Tokyo to thank them for their help, and the Matsukatas had become interested in the work she was planning to do in Kuji. Takeshi had never met them nor visited in their home, but he got directions from a nearby police box and presented himself at the Matsukata residence.

When I got to their home, I found a room just filled with beautifully dressed Japanese women. They wanted me to talk and to tell them about the work. They knew that Miss Allen was interned, and they thought that we must be suffering up our way. They asked how we were faring and what Christian work we were trying to do. I wasn't used to talking to women in that way, but I did the very best I could. Although I was embarrassed, I told them what we were trying to do.

The women listened to Takeshi until it was time for lunch. They invited him to join them, and he enjoyed the first real meal that he had had in a long time. After lunch he talked again, and they listened thoughtfully to all that he had to say. At last they told him that they had been very much impressed by his story and by the work which he was trying to do. They told him that they would give him 3,000 yen for the year's work, with 1,000 yen to take back with him, the rest promised later. Almost overwhelmed, Takeshi took the bills and tucked them away carefully. He learned, as he talked to them, that one reason for their proffered assistance was their discouragement with many of the Christian leaders who had given up any attempt at Christian work in the face of police pressure. "Through your trials you have stayed firm and have not given up," they told him.

But this was not the end of the help which Takeshi received from the Matsukata family. As he became better acquainted with Mr. Shokuma Matsukata, he realized that he had much to learn about agriculture and finance, and he saw that Mr. Matsukata knew a great deal about both.

"During all the war years Mr. and Mrs. Matsukata stood by us loyally and efficiently," Takeshi wrote, "and I don't know what in the world we would have done without them. God certainly raised them up to demonstrate his love here."

Takeshi also found help in the friendship of Merrell Vories. After the completion of the Center building, work had been started on a house for Tommy, but it was not finished at the outbreak of the war. When it was completed, the construction foreman from the Omi Brotherhood refused to turn over the keys to Takeshi until all of the money had been paid. Takeshi explained that many people were leaving the cities; women and children were moving to the country to escape the threat of air raids, and every inch of housing was needed. But the overseer was adamant; no money, no keys. Finally Takeshi set out for Tokyo to consult Merrell Vories.

Mr. Vories, his wife, and his mother had been exiled from the Brotherhood and had settled in a small home in Tokyo. When Takeshi arrived at their home, they were at breakfast and insisted that he share their meal. Takeshi, who had had only three potatoes during the sixteen-hour trip, was grateful for a warm meal. They asked him about the work in Kuji and how he happened to be in Tokyo, and he explained that since there was a debt of 1,600 yen on the house, he could not obtain possession of it.

Mr. and Mrs. Vories glanced at each other and then turned to Takeshi. They explained that they had been dismissed from the Omi Brotherhood and no longer had anything to say about its policies; but, just the evening before they had received a money order containing "tear money," or severance pay, and the amount was exactly 1,600 yen. They had talked about the money and decided that it was a special fund which must not be used for personal expenses, but for some particular project instead. "And maybe, just maybe, the first person who comes tomorrow will be the one who needs it." Taking out the envelope, Mr. Vories handed it to Takeshi. "Now you take this as a gift from God," he said. "It isn't a debt, and Miss Allen needn't ever pay it back; it's a gift."

Filled with deep gratitude and awe, Takeshi returned to Kuji, paid off the overseer, and obtained possession of the house which was soon filled with refugees.

Shortly after the war broke out, there was a drive to collect scrap metal, and the police came to Kuni, suggesting that she contribute the hinges and door knobs, the window frames and the other metal fittings of the buildings. After receiving them courteously and listening quietly to their demands, she replied: "Yes, I'll be glad to give you all of the door knobs and metal that you want, but first I'm sure you will give all of the door knobs and hinges from the government buildings. After you take them and use them, then come back here and we'll give you these."

The town burned during the war, but it was not from enemy action; Japanese towns have often burned from a spark on the tatami or a cinder on dry wood. Hundreds of townspeople were without homes, and the Center offered them shelter and shared their rations with them. Again the local officials came to Kuni, saying that they needed the building to use for city offices. She asked for time to think over their request, and they agreed to come back the following day. On their return Kuni said that she had decided to give them the building rent free; however, there were a few rules to which they must agree to conform: No nails were to be driven into the walls, there was to be no smoking in the building, and, if tables and chairs were used, cotton must be applied to the legs in order to protect the floors. The officials left at once to locate their offices elsewhere.

The most serious threat came late in the war after Takeshi had been recalled to the Army, but he was home on leave when he learned that the military had decided to take over the building. He realized that this was a different problem from that of dealing with local politicians, and he immediately sought out the commanding officer, asking permission to take off his uniform jacket and speak to him as a civilian. After the commanding officer gave his permission, Takeshi told him the history of the Center and explained the sense of responsibility which he felt for the building.

"This building was given by a woman in America who is a fine Christian, and she gave the money for the express purpose of extending Christianity. How can I give you permission to take over the Center for any other use?"

The officer replied, "Suppose we take it without your permission; suppose we just seize the building. You know that we can do that."

"Yes," said Takeshi, "yes, I know you can, but I would rather burn it to the ground than to have it used in any way other than for the purpose for which it was given." Reminded he would face prison or death if he did burn the building, Takeshi continued, "I know I'll be put in prison, and I don't mind that; but I *do* mind having this building used in any other way than for Christian purposes."

There was a long pause as Takeshi picked up his jacket and put it on. Now he was a soldier again, subject to military law and at the mercy of his senior officer. He waited, cap in hand, for whatever blow might fall. The officer stared at him, and then he shrugged and said, "You may go." Nothing more was said about confiscation of the building.

Gnawing hunger and constant cold were hard to bear, but the suspicion and hostility of their neighbors were even harder to take. Takeshi recalls:

No one ever came to see us, and no one spoke; we were absolutely alone. People would meet us on the street, people who had been our friends, but no one ever dared to speak. However, when I say that, I have to make one notable exception. In a little village about forty miles from here, a mountain town with no railroad, there was a school teacher, Miss Kamiiwa. She had had tuberculosis of the bone and had lost one leg by amputation. Although she tried many religions to see if she could not find spiritual help, nothing did any good, and she was most depressed and downcast.

When her father was a young man, he had heard an itinerant missionary tell the story of the Prodigal Son. He didn't remember much about it, except that there was a religion such as Christianity that taught that God was the father of all. Knowing that we were Christians, she came to talk with us one day, and from that time on, she did not miss one single week. She was our only contact with the outside world up here, the only one who dared to come to see us. There was no transportation except by a truck which came to Kuji once a week in the early morning. She rode that truck out in the open through wind, rain, or snow, and she came every weekend. Finally Miss Kamiiwa became a Christian. As you watch her face today, it is aglow with the peace and joy that are in her heart.

Every Sunday Takeshi held church services for the household, but no one other than Miss Kamiiwa dared to attend. "But I knew that God was there with us, and those very, very small services meant a great deal to me."

The birth of the child, Junko, in 1944 brought joy to the household, but it increased the problems which they were already facing. Kuni was ill after Junko was born, and it was two years before she recovered. Takeshi tried to find a doctor, but there were none in Kuji, and when he talked to a doctor in a village many miles away, the man refused to come. The only help he was able to secure was an injection of medicine supplied by a friendly nurse. Nor could he get milk for the child, for the few farmers with dairy cattle refused to sell him any milk. After scouring the countryside, he finally found a man who was willing to supply one third of a pint each day, and with that the baby began to grow. Then Takeshi located a few boxes of cereal which Tommy had left behind, and he carefully picked out the worms with which they were infested and used the cereal to feed the baby.

In March, 1945, Takeshi was drafted into the Army and sent south to a camp near Sendai. Behind him he left an invalid wife, a seven-months old baby, and two women. "Then too, by that time, the draft meant almost certain death. It was a very difficult time, and yet we never gave up hope — never," he recalls.

Shortly after he arrived in camp, Takeshi had to attend a lecture on religion and hear an officer explaining that Christianity was selfish, for a Christian man cared for nothing except his own personal salvation. There was no place in Japan, he said, for such a selfish creed. But Takeshi promptly challenged his interpretation:

Your facts are not right; you gave the wrong impression in your talk to the soldiers. You talked about the gods of Japan and spoke of the Emperor as a god, but our God, the Christian God, is the creator of the universe. None of the Japanese gods created the universe, not even the Emperor. There's one true God in Christianity,

the creator God. And besides, it is not a selfish religion. Society
is made up of individuals, and of course the individual *is* precious
in God's sight; but the value of Christian faith is in one individual
helping another, and that person helping and telling someone else
until all society becomes Christian. It is most unselfish and not
selfish as you say.

Again Takeshi escaped imprisonment and punishment, and
eventually he earned the friendship and goodwill of the lecturer.

In the spring of 1945 there was an air of desperation in Japan,
for imperial Tokyo presented a strange and dreadful spectacle.
A complex of modern concrete buildings in the heart of the city
still stood around the palace moat, and far out in the suburbs
there was a ring of homes as yet untouched by fire. Between the
two lay acres of ashes, rubble, twisted iron, and free-standing
chimneys. Few reminders of war are more poignant than a
chimney, once the heart of a home, standing alone in the midst
of desolation. Nothing could now conceal from the people the
fact that they were facing invasion. In Kuji the women were
issued bamboo sticks, and they practiced bayoneting with the
sharp bamboo. The older men dug caves in the hills and prepared to defend the coast to the best of their ability.

Kuni and her sisters watched Junko cling precariously to her
hard-bought existence, and they knew that their own strength
was ebbing with that of the nation. In the jungles of New Guinea
Kozo Yahaba struggled to feed the fever-ridden troops who were
cut off completely from the home islands and gave up hope of
seeing Japan again. Takeshi was chosen to be a human torpedo
and pilot a small wooden boat equipped with dynamite to the
hull of an enemy ship for detonation. And in Tule Lake Tommy
listened to the radio, prayerfully following the rumors and
counter-rumors that were broadcast during the summer.

On August 6 the nuclear age was born in a flash of light and
a mushroom cloud which obliterated the city of Hiroshima. Three
days later a second atomic bomb fell on the city of Nagasaki.

Commander Masatake Okumiya, who was in command of
Japan's home island air defense, was one of the first men to
arrive at Hiroshima. He had left Tokyo as soon as reports of the
Hiroshima bombing reached General Headquarters, and he had

landed at Iwakuni Naval Air Base on August 7. Early on the morning of August 8 he reached Hiroshima. He reported:

> Nothing—neither films, magazines, books, eloquent speeches— nothing can possibly express to any other person except those actual witnesses at Hiroshima what happened to the city and what occurred after the bomb fell. It was an appalling spectacle beyond the power of words to describe. Cold printed or celluloid media cannot carry the sounds and smells and "feelings" of that shattered city.[6]

A week later a million hands tuned the radios of Japan, and a million heads bent reverently to hear the voice of their Emperor announcing "an extraordinary measure":

> To our good and loyal subjects:
> After pondering deeply the general trends of the world and the actual conditions obtaining in our Empire today, we have decided to effect a settlement of the present situation by resorting to an extraordinary measure.
> We have ordered Our Government to communicate to the Governments of the United States, Great Britain, China and the Soviet Union that Our Empire accepts the provisions of their Joint Declaration. . . .

Peace had come.

[6] Masatake Okumiya and Jiro Horikoshi with Martin Caidin, *Zero!* New York: E. P. Dutton & Co., Inc., 1956, p. 391.

Chapter Twelve

TO BUILD AND TO PLANT

WHEN THE WAR WAS OVER, there was no way to describe the condition of Japan; the circumstances were terrible. There was nothing to buy in the stores, and everyone was hungry. Takeshi came back home and spent days in prayer, trying to discover what he could do for his town; how to help get Japan on her feet again; how to show Japan the spiritual mistakes she had made; how to make human beings out of people who had become almost the opposite.

Takeshi returned to Kuji thankful that his wife, his child, and his wife's sisters had lived through the war, but wondering what the future held for his countrymen. Of his brother Kozo he had no news, yet he hoped that somehow Kozo might have survived the war, and might yet return to Japan.

Struggling against physical exhaustion, against hunger, and against the paralyzing shock of defeat, the Japanese people withstood the first winter. Shacks constructed of salvaged wood, battered tin, and packing boxes were built on land cleared of rubble and ashes. Tiny gardens grew green in the spring of 1946, and as the little shoots colored the black earth, sprouts of hope began to brighten the outlook of the people.

Under the American Occupation the machinery of constitutional government began to function again. Military government teams were established in local centers throughout Japan to work with prefectural and local governments. Contact between the American teams and the Japanese began to allay the people's fears of the conquerors' intentions. The bamboo spears and the

M-1 rifles were laid aside, and tentative efforts at grass roots friendship began on both sides.

Even isolated Kuji became accustomed to the sight of American troops, and Kuni found herself unexpectedly popular after years of ostracism. She became accustomed to answering frantic calls from officials who could not understand what the English-speaking soldiers wished to tell them. Shortly after the occupation began, she had a cautious American soldier as a house guest.

One of the soldiers came and wanted to stay all night, so I let him stay in our house. When I fixed his bed for him, he put his gun right at his head, and he put all of his valuables in a little bag and kept that at his head, too. I didn't think it was odd; I thought it was normal, for these should be a soldier's precautions. We had been the enemy, and naturally he would fear and mistrust us. However, when he left, he asked us to keep a box of food for him until he came back the next time, and I put it away carefully. It was months before he returned, but when he did come, I at once brought out that box of food that he had left. The soldier was surprised and delighted, and he knew that we were trustworthy and honest. After that when he stayed with us, he left his gun around any old place.

On another occasion a troop of thirty young soldiers came seeking a place where they might spend the night. None of the officials understood what the American soldiers wanted, so they hurried off to find Kuni and to bring her to the town to speak to the Americans. When she learned that they wanted to stay all night, she told them that they could spend the night in the Center building. At first they refused, assuring her that they were used to sleeping outside; but when she again offered to fix their beds in the building, they accepted.

They were so surprised to see this beautiful building with hard-wood floors, and when we brought them a large mosquito net, they were very grateful. One thing I noticed right then and there: These American soldiers were very different from the Japanese. In getting the net up, the Japanese soldiers would have pounded nails into the wall, and they wouldn't have thought a thing about it. But the American boys did not drive any nails anywhere; they put up the net without a single nail. I knew then that these soldiers had received good home training and were quite different from Japanese soldiers. We also gave them some records to play on the record player. When they saw chairs in my house, they just couldn't get over it, but they sat on them and enjoyed it thoroughly. The next morning the soldiers took the net down, and they folded it up very nicely even though they are not easy to fold. Again, I was filled with thankfulness that they had had such lovely home training. I'd like for their mothers to know about it; they were so careful of other people, and they were careful of other people's things.

During the first year of the occupation, only the necessary military personnel or civilians were permitted to live in Japan. The suffering Japanese church needed the help of the American church, and American churchmen were eager to respond, but the occupation authorities had to proceed cautiously; they had to avoid violating their own principles of freedom of religion in reinstating the foreign mission program. In addition, they could hardly bring in missionaries as part of the occupation program, and neither could they allow foreigners to return and burden the already strained Japanese economy.

In 1947, Tommy received permission to return to Japan. She knew from Kuni's letters that the entire northern area was destitute, and that clothing, food, rubber boots, and blankets were needed. In anticipation of her return she gathered together "tons and tons of relief materials." A friendly chaplain helped her to send some of the goods to Japan by taking a shipment with his personal baggage, and she was able to take some with her. Another friend in Tokyo accepted the chaplain's consignment.

 My friend had not bargained for so much! A soldier who was with her at the time said to her, "What on earth are you going to do with all those boxes?" When my friend said she didn't know, the soldier replied, "Well, I'm in the transportation department, and I will see that they all get up to Kuji for you." And so it worked out just like that; all the things were sent up to Kuji. They met such a great need because the people had been without goods for so very long.

When Tommy reached Kuji early in 1947, she, who had left under police escort, found herself welcomed by the entire population of the town. "I found myself quite popular, and I wasn't used to that!" The Center played a useful role in securing and distributing relief supplies, and shortly after her return Tommy wrote to friends in the United States:

Would that all the churches, societies, groups, and individuals who so generously gave clothing, food, supplies, and money for our needs could witness the joy and gratitude of the recipients. Life has been one continual sharing since my return; sharing with repatriates from Manchuria, sharing with Christian workers and their families, and sharing with friends far and near. A mother wrote me a letter of thanks the other day, saying that her little four-year-old boy was so happy over his "new" clothes that he got up in the middle of the night to try them on again. He was a war baby, so he had never had such fine clothes before.

Conditions in Japan slowly improved, for careful rationing and the import of food insured the physical survival of the Japanese people; powdered milk saved a generation of babies. With the advice and consent of the occupation, general elections were held, and the Diet began to test its increased powers. There was an openness to new ideas in the country, and there was an eagerness to learn about things American. Even in the far north, the patient women and the tired farmers breathed the heady air of freedom and talked of democracy. But physical improvement and political freedom did not solve the moral and ideological vacuum in which the nation drifted.

In May, 1947, Tommy and Takeshi were invited to be the guests of honor at a double celebration held in a little mountain town forty miles from Kuji. The town had built its first junior high school building and used the occasion to dedicate the school and recognize the revised constitution at the same time. Transportation for the guests of honor was a rickety, crowded charcoal-burning bus, and when Tommy looked at it, she began to doubt the wisdom of the trip.

 When I saw people getting on the bus, climbing in the windows and hanging on at every conceivable angle, I thought to myself, "I just cannot do it; I can never get on." But we had to get on, and the man in charge of the buses told the driver that he must save a seat for us, and get us to our destination on time, even if he had to use precious gasoline to get up the hills. So, sitting in front and holding on for dear life, we climbed up and over the worst roads imaginable. In between the bumps and bruises I managed to cast fleeting glances at the cherry and plum trees in full bloom and to think about the kindness of the people around me and of their uncomplaining way of accepting the bumps and bruises of life.

It took the rickety bus four hours to travel the forty miles, but they reached their destination. There they found that forty young men and women had gathered and were waiting in a large upper room, hoping for an extra evening meeting. In their minds were a thousand and one questions: What is American democracy? Will it work in Japan? How did American women function in a democracy? What can we do to help make a new Japan? What is the relation between science and religion? Tell us about Christianity. Explain your educational system.

Well, we got so interested in trying to answer some of these "little" questions that we talked until midnight, quite forgetting the bruises of the ride.

The following morning the official celebration took place. On a platform decked with red and white bunting, the mayor and the town leaders spoke, expressing their sense of guilt and their hopes for a new, democratic Japan. In the afternoon the school was dedicated, and the principal said in his address:

"I know that Miss Allen's heart aches when she sees the impoverished condition of our people, but we want her to know that if Japan and Germany had won this war, our situation under a fascist regime would have been intolerable. We have been saved from that, and now America is giving us a chance to make a new Japan, and we are grateful. Please thank your people, and tell them that we want and need friends—we are lonely for friends."

Sensing the opportunity to reach villagers who had never before been open to the ideas of democracy and the doctrines of Christianity, Tommy felt a desperate need to extend the work beyond the boundaries of Kuji.

One of our missionaries once said, "We pray God to bless our work, and then, when he does, we are greatly troubled." How very true! Our budgets have a way of remaining stationary while the work grows, the needs multiply, and one spends anxious hours considering ways to meet the increased opportunities.

In 1948 Tommy had opportunity to demonstrate the need for some means of transportation in her work to two prominent Baptist visitors from the United States.

I took both of them to Karumai in one of the charcoal-burning buses. The roads between here and Karumai were simply terrible, and we hit our heads against the ceiling almost every other minute. Then the conductor said, "From now on you must be careful, for the roads will be bad!" Although we all laughed over that, my two friends felt that our greatest need was a sturdy station wagon with four-wheel drive. Nothing else would get us over the roads or, rather, the lack of roads here. So from Portland, Oregon, and from Calvary Church in Washington, D. C., a beautiful station wagon came to us and made it possible for us to do more extensive work in different villages.

Two American military bases were located near Kuji; one was Camp Haugen, about three hours away in the town of Hachinohe, and the other was Misawa Air Base, about five hours from Kuji. American soldiers and airmen learned, to their surprise, that there was an American missionary living in Kuji in an American home, and they became frequent visitors.

One time when quite a group came, I happened to be ironing, and I had things strewn over the house. When I apologized for the way the house looked, they said, "Oh, but it looks just like home!" I think the mothers would be pleased to know that their sons felt right at home in my house!

American missionaries lived a somewhat ambiguous life under the occupation. They were not entitled to the privileges accorded military and civilian personnel of official status, yet they were American citizens interested in the success of the occupation, and representatives of the professed religion of the majority of United States citizens. Warmhearted soldiers and chaplains often assisted the missionaries in ways that were morally defensible, if not always entirely in accord with military regulations.

One day I was riding on the military train as a guest of the American government. I had gone down to Tokyo and was coming back, and this was the best way to travel. The other trains were just awful, and you could scarcely get on them, anyway. I considered that I was an American citizen, that in many ways I was working for democracy, and that my own government would be glad for me to ride on their military trains. So I got on, but naturally I didn't have any military money. I wondered how I was ever going to get anything to eat because the dining car which served the soldiers and the officers accepted only military coin. So I thought, "Well, I'll just have to go without food for two or three meals until I get back home to Kuji."

Early the next morning everybody else was going in for

breakfast, and the Japanese car boy asked, "Aren't you going in to breakfast?" "No, I'm not," I replied. "I don't have any military money." "Oh," he said, "We have such a nice steward, I'm sure he'll do something about it." "Oh, no, please don't do anything about it," I begged. But he came back after awhile and said, "You're a missionary, aren't you?" When I said "Yes," he continued, "The steward says for you to come right on in; you can eat all you want, and it won't cost you a thing." Well, I thought that was lovely, although I was quite hesitant about doing it; but he insisted, so I went, and I thanked the steward very warmly. I thought perhaps I'd better eat enough breakfast to last me the rest of the day, because I didn't know when I'd get any more food, so I ate a big breakfast and thanked him again.

When I went back to my seat I heard someone call "Miss Allen, what are you doing here?" I wondered what was going to happen to me, but here was one of the officers from the military government in Morioka. I told him, "You're the answer to a maiden's prayer, for I'd like to borrow a dollar to pay for my breakfast and to buy lunch before I get back to Kuji. I'll pay you back." He had been a guest in my home, and said, "All right, but keep the dollar. I've been over to your house and I'll be coming again."

So I took the money and went back into the dining car at noon and offered to pay for my breakfast and buy some lunch, telling the steward, "I've got some money now." But he said, "No, no, I won't take your money. You just keep it, and here's your lunch." So instead of having to fast the whole trip, I enjoyed two big meals and was a dollar to the good.

Thirty-three years had passed since Tommy had first set out for Japan; she had studied the language, she had taught for ten years, and she had spent another ten years working in and around Morioka. The war had shattered her first plans for Kuji, but the peace had given her a second chance. It had been ten years since Tommy had first moved to Kuji in 1938, and the shy kindergarteners who had come to a small, dark room to sit on tangerine crates were now tall boys and girls in high school uniforms. Immediate needs had been met, the relief crisis was past, and Japan was returning to normal. It was time to look ahead.

 I found two verbs in the first chapter of Jeremiah [RSV] which came to me with new force. The tenth verse called Jeremiah "to pluck up and to break down, to destroy and to overthrow, to build and to plant." *To build and to plant!* How profound! What must we build? Character, the church, the Christian community, the Kingdom of God? What shall we plant, and where? The land must be prepared, and the means must be found. These two little commands include everything. We must start where we are and work out our own answers in the framework of our own lives. No matter how many fine blueprints there are for programs and policies, it often comes to the individual to decide in the end, and yet that is not the entire answer, either.

It seemed to Tommy the time to move ahead, for there were assets upon which future work could be built. First of all, in the country meetings the audiences were receptive and open-minded. Conservative farmers and fishermen and shopkeepers and businessmen may change slowly and accept new ideas gradually, but they admire courage. Tommy's willingness to stay in Kuji until she was interned and the steadfast Christian witness of the Yahabas during the war had not gone unnoticed by the people there. And they were also aware of the dedication of Kuni and Takeshi. Takeshi's earlier spiritual struggles had resolved themselves into a firm wartime witness which had left neither his patriotism nor his Christianity in doubt. Kuni's faith, which had matured more gently, was both deep and intellectual. There was no question as to their ability to direct the Center, for not only was their faith tried and proven, but they brought their practical gifts to the work, as well. Tommy explained their roles: "Kuni does the planning, Takeshi does the executing, and I do the worrying."

Kozo Yahaba, missing for many months after the surrender, was finally located in a Dutch prisoner-of-war camp. When he was able to return to Japan, he went at once to Kuji to see his older brother and to ask for baptism. This was a great joy to Takeshi. He had first glimpsed the possibilities of Christianity when he stood, tired and grimy, in a small bookstore and read the story of Zaccheus. He had noted then that not only was Zaccheus changed by his sudden meeting with Jesus Christ, but all of his household as well. Kozo had hoped to become a doctor, but his dreams of a medical career were casualties of the war. Now he had come to share the vision of his brother, and he decided to commit his life to service in Kuji. To prepare for his work, he attended the new Rural Training and Service Institute which had been established in Hino Machi near Tokyo by the United Church of Christ in Japan.

Kuni's two sisters, Kimi and Tsuyako, had been educated at Shokei, in Sendai; and they had both received further educational training in Tokyo and had joined her in Kuji. After Kozo Yahaba cast his lot with the enterprise at Kuji, he and Tsuyako Obara were married, and the ceremony was the first Christian wedding ever held in the area.

There were open doors in Kuji, and there were people ready and willing to walk through them, but new developments cost money. Fortunately, the Center had one other asset, Tommy's gift for making Kuji and its needs real to other people. Speaking and writing, she communicated not only a steadfast and mystical faith, but also a concern for the practical things of daily life and a leavening sense of humor, all of which are suggested in these incidents:

Once when she was scheduled to speak to a group of American women in Tokyo, her old friend, Mr. William Woodard, listened to the announcement of the coming meeting, and then he rose to urge the women not to miss the program. "But," he added, "when Tommy speaks, leave the rent money at home!" She welcomed the inquiries of an Army chaplain in Japan by informing him that she felt "a chaplain ought to be interested in Christian work." Then Tommy assured an American audience that she enjoyed speaking in the United States, "because you can always find a few Christians in American churches."

An old friend and fellow missionary told of being deeply touched as she listened to Tommy's harrowing and dramatic description of a bitterly cold week-end in Kuji. It was so cold that she had to wear two pairs of woolen gloves to do her housework, and she found the eggs in her kitchen frozen solid. "Then," said the friend, "just as she reached the most harrowing part of the story, I suddenly remembered that I had visited her that week-end. It *was* cold, and the eggs *did* freeze, but we were having so much fun that neither of us noticed it!"

Another friend, a childhood comrade from Franklin, Indiana, wrote Tommy that she was remembering Kuji in her will. She laughed until she wept over the letter she received in reply. Tommy's answer was brief and to the point, "Oh good! When are you going to die?"

Speaking of one group of church women, Tommy described an experience of faith during the war years when she saw love and faith calm a storm. At that time she was interned with a mother and two children in Morioka, and late one night a terrible storm struck the town. As the wind howled, the wooden shutters banged, and the timbers of the house creaked menacingly. Rain beat against the walls of the building and shattered against the trees as the fury of the storm mounted. Terrified and almost hysterical with fear, one of the children came to her mother, weeping and sobbing. The mother comforted the little girl, soothed and calmed her, and took her into her own bed. Snuggled in bed with her mother, the child said with a sigh of relief, "Now the storm is over!" The wind still howled, and the rain still fell in torrents; but for that child, the storm had ended.

Neither Tommy nor Kuni nor Takeshi ever doubted that they must move ahead, not trying to blueprint the ultimate development of the work, but rather, seeking to move as the needs of Kuji suggested. Tommy's efforts to expand the Center to cope with the religious and social problems of Kuji moved her outside of the regular paths of organized mission work and into a role of considerable independence. The strength of the post-war witness of the Center had justified the chance she had taken in moving to Kuji and in staying there until 1941, as well as the chances which the Yahabas had taken during the war. It looked as if the opportunities ahead were too great to be bypassed in an effort to gain security. Tommy was, after all, the child of a mother who never let financial needs interfere with her tithe to the Lord's Purse.

As the Center grew and developed during the years between 1950 and 1960, Tommy often had to remind herself that the Lord had promised Jeremiah that "as He had watched over the overthrowing and the destruction, so would He also watch over the building and the planting."

Chapter Thirteen

A CHURCH FOR MR. OSANAI

Thus says the Lord:
   "The people who survived the sword
   Found grace in the wilderness. . . ."

Jeremiah 31:2 (RSV)

AT LAST THE LONG YEARS OF WORK, the hours of teaching and witnessing, the miles of hiking up and down the roads of Iwate Ken, and the steadfast faith of the war years bore fruit. On September 26, 1948, the first baptismal service was held in Kuji, and fifteen believers gathered at the river for Christian baptism; again, on Christmas day, fourteen believers were baptized. Many of these new Christians were deeply troubled, for their lives had been shattered by the war, but they found something in Christianity which they had sought in other faiths and had not found.

 From seven in the evening till after midnight on Christmas Eve, we listened to the stories and confessions of faith of the fourteen to be baptized. They were so thrilling; it made us forget the time as each person described his struggles and victory in detail. One disillusioned ex-soldier told how he had turned to Buddhism to find the answer to his problems, but he found it not; then he had turned to the study of Communism, but the answer was not there; but he did find what he was seeking in Jesus. A war widow, a young woman who had lost her husband in the bombing at Hiroshima, had returned with her baby to Kuji, her former home; but in her sorrow she had found peace in Jesus. Christianity was something new, real, and challenging to each convert, and it made some of us older ones feel very humble indeed.

110

That same glad Christmas day, the church was organized, and the membership made two important decisions: The first was to sponsor evangelistic work in a neighboring town, and the second was to start a church building fund, designating a certain number of offerings each year. As the tiny building fund grew, the church members met in the library of the Center building, where on Sunday mornings the pastor stood before a simple lectern to speak to his earnest congregation. On the wall behind him was a picture illustrating the Great Commission and a simple wooden cross, the gift of the Union Church of the Tule Lake Relocation Center. Tastefully-arranged flowers, greens, or autumn leaves completed the atmosphere of worship. Within a few years after the founding of the Kuji Church Tommy could write with satisfaction, "The center and unifier of all of our activities is the church."

Among the members of the Kuji church is Mr. Sado Osanai, resident of the village of Kawai located about twelve miles away. He is typical of the young farmers who have had the courage and the ambition to break with the three-thousand-year-old farming methods, and he has hope for the future of his village and of his farm; but his greatest hope is in the new life he has found in Christianity.

Mr. Osanai's own village is one of the tiny hamlets that dot the north with hardly more than four or five houses in each, hamlets that were largely cut off from contact with the outside world until after World War II. Here, for seven hundred years, the Osanai family has farmed the same tiny plot of land. His mother sweeps the yard with a bamboo broom just as her grandmother swept the same yard, and, when it rains, she slips on a straw raincoat like the ones worn by generations of Japanese farmers. His home is an L-shaped building of the Nambu architecture, a style characteristic of homes in the Nambu fief. For seventy years the house has stood in Kawai; for seventy years charcoal fires have burned in the fire pits; and for seventy years their smoke has blackened the beams and the ceiling. Around the house lie tiny fields which the family has farmed for several generations, and above the house, on the mountainside, is a lean-to kiln for burning charcoal. It is not an easy thing for a man in a rural village to change his way of life, and it is an even harder thing for a young man to face his parents and ask for permission to make a change in their way of life.

But several years ago Mr. Osanai attended one of the Farmers' Gospel Schools held at the Kuji Center. Like the other young men he shared the dormitory life and enjoyed the fellowship. He brought his own bedding and slept in the loft of the barn where it was clean and warm and dry. He ate from rough, wooden tables built by the carpenter, but Kuni's garlands of green leaves made them seem beautiful. He listened to talks by agricultural authorities, he watched demonstrations of new farming and dairying practices, and, as he saw the results, hope dawned in his life.

Mr. Osanai had two friends in the village who had also attended the Farmers' Gospel School, and together they began to talk of selling their work horses and buying dairy cattle. At last, after much study of the dairy industry and after a great deal of discussion and explanation, they took the big step and bought dairy cows. The income from the milk of Mr. Osanai's two sleek and carefully tended cows gave the family a little extra margin of profit. Soon fertilizer began to restore the seven-hundred-year-old fields, and the crops began to improve; *hope had matured and had produced results.*

But faith was also a part of the new ideas introduced at the Farmers' Gospel School, a different kind of a faith; one which spoke of a creator God, a God with a purpose and a steadfast love for all humanity. According to this faith, God had given man, even the village farmer, dominion over his environment and expected him to make use of it for the benefit of himself and all other men. This was a very different teaching from the traditional concept of life in harmony with the natural environment. Mr. Osanai began to study the Bible which recorded the mighty acts of this God in history, and he began to understand that there was a place for him in God's plans, a place that only he could fill.

Christmas was coming, and he began to hope that it would come to Kawai. "Would it be possible," he asked Mr. Yahaba, "to have a Christmas in the village, a Christmas in his home?" Takeshi agreed to come, and Mr. Osanai and his friends told the village children about the program that they would see. But he had one problem, that of telling his family about the new things that were happening to him. He had to have their permission for the Christmas program, and he hoped he might also have their understanding. His hard-working mother cared little one way or the other, for her world of drudgery in the house and in the field left her with little time or inclination to appreciate her son's ideas. Mr. Osanai's father also had little sympathy with the new notions of his son and his friends; in his own narrow world he had found stimulation and release from his troubles in drinking more and more heavily. However, he gave permission for the meeting to be held in the Osanai home and grudgingly agreed not to drink on the day of Christmas out of courtesy to the visitors.

When the great day came, one hundred children from Kawai and nearby villages gathered for their part of the program. A gay little tree sparkled in the gloom of the smoke-blackened room, and a lavish use of charcoal took some of the chill off of the frosty air. There were stories and songs for the children, as well as a sack of candy and a Christmas card for each one.

At nine o'clock the children's Christmas party ended, and the older ones started for home while the others curled up to nap while their parents talked. Then Takeshi Yahaba started to speak to the forty adults gathered in the Osanai home, and for two hours he talked to a rapt audience, telling the simple story of the birth of the Christ Child and what the event had meant to the world. Then he told of Christ's coming into his life and heart, what it had meant to him, and what it could mean to other men. No one listened more closely or more carefully than Mr. Osanai's father, for human problems and suffering are much the same the world over. As the old man listened, a change began to come over him, and the same night, after the guests had gone and they were alone together, he told his son, "If that is what Christianity is and does, I will withdraw my objection to your baptism."

Discipleship did not come easily to Mr. Osanai, and up until the very moment of his baptism the road to Christianity continued to be a rugged one for him. Easter was the date set for the service, and it was to be held in a stream near the Kuji

Center. He was up early, caring for his cows, doing the chores, and anticipating the events of the day. Up on the mountain stood the lean-to where he burned charcoal, and at the last minute he had some work to do at the kiln. As he worked, he saw, to his horror, the one daily bus go down the road and disappear in the direction of Kuji, twelve miles distant! He knew he would be late, but he determined that he would get to Kuji. Three hours later, after running and walking the twelve miles through the gorge and over the mountains, he reached the Center and was baptized. As he shared in the Communion experience which followed his baptism, he knew that *faith, too, had matured and produced results.*

And as Tommy shared Communion with the church members and thought of the war-torn lives and agonizing decisions, words from Jeremiah came unbidden to her mind: "Keep your voice from weeping, and your eyes from tears; for your work shall be rewarded, says the Lord, and they shall come back from the land of the enemy."

Before the First Baptist Church of Kuji was a year old, it found itself facing two knotty problems, the denominational affiliation of the new church and the ordination of its pastor. In 1940 the churches related to the American Baptist societies had joined the Kyodan, United Church of Christ in Japan, which was formed at that time; and, in 1948, the Baptist churches were still a part of the United Church.

The rules of church government, drawn up in 1948, established standards for the admission of church bodies and for the licensing and ordination of pastors. Several types of church bodies were recognized, and requirements were established for their classification. A first-class church, Dai-ishu, had to have at least forty communicant members, an ordained pastor, and the financial ability to pay the pastoral salary, to support the church program, and to assume its share of the budget of the national church. A second-class church, Dai-nishu, required a minimum of twenty members, an ordained pastor, and a monthly budget of an amount specified by the United Church. If a group could not meet these qualifications, it could not be recognized as a church; but it could affiliate with the United Church as a Dendosho, or Evangelism Station. There were no specified require-ments as to its membership or financial responsibility; the only standard essential was responsible pastoral oversight.

On application to the Tohoku Kyoku, or Northern District of the United Church, the Kuji Church discovered that it could be recognized only as a Dendosho. The membership believed that they should be recognized as a church, but the chances of a rural church in a small town meeting the financial requirements placed on first- and second-class churches were slim. Urban churches could meet financial responsibilities beyond the capabilities of rural churches.

Ordination by the Kyodan required a theological examination, and Takeshi did not feel that he could subscribe to the concept of the church as defined by the United Church. He felt that he was qualified through training and practical experience, but he had a certain independence of spirit which had led him from the Episcopal Church. This spirit had become even stronger during the loneliness of his work in Kuji, and had been tempered by his repeated clashes during the war with political and military au-thority.

The Kuji Church decided against affiliation with the United Church and made plans for congregational ordination. Notices to this effect were sent out by the church, and in December, 1951, Takeshi was ordained. Four Baptist missionaries, serving as dele-gates from their churches, and an American Army chaplain per-formed the service of ordination on behalf of the congregation.

The date chosen, December 8, was (according to the Japanese calendar) the anniversary of Pearl Harbor, the beginning of war and of Tommy's internment. As she watched Takeshi kneel for the service and glanced at the intent faces of the membership as well as the American delegates, Tommy felt that reconcilia-tion was complete.

Those cherished Baptist principles, religious freedom, congre-gational polity, and the concept of the church as a fellowship of believers, present difficulties whenever Baptists face the ques-tion of denominational union. Japanese Baptist churches have struggled with these issues ever since the formation of the United Church of Christ in Japan in 1940.

Announcement of the newly formed United Church of Christ in Japan was made under dramatic circumstances. The year 1940 was the 2600th year since the accession of the legendary first emperor of Japan, Jimmu Tenno; and Jimmu Tenno Day, October 17, was the occasion for a nationwide celebration. Thousands of people gathered for the ceremony on the campus of the Methodist School, Aoyama Gakuin, in Tokyo. Here the climax of a long day of speeches and sermons came with the reading of a manifesto, pledging Christians to greater efforts during the national emergency and announcing the uniting of the churches into one national body. Most of the churches in Japan were thus forged into one ecclesiastical body, and in this form they endured the war years. After the war the New Religious Bodies Law was revoked, and a new constitutional article guaranteeing religious freedom was adopted.

The American Baptist Foreign Mission Society and the Woman's American Baptist Foreign Mission Society did not join in the Interboard Committee,[7] but continued their relationships with the Baptist churches which were now a part of the United Church. For several years most Baptist churches remained a part of the United Church, although they also formed their own association, the Shinsei Kai. Beginning in 1949, a yearly general meeting was held, and a Central Committee was organized to guide the reconstruction program, to meet personnel problems, to deal with Baptist schools, and to assume some responsibility for the administration of funds for rebuilding schools and churches. Organizational relationships were decidedly complex; problems of ordination, theological training, and church government plagued the churches. The adoption of a creed by the United Church in 1954 was opposed by some Baptist leaders and supported by others.

Both Japanese Baptists and American Baptist missionaries found it difficult to work under the ambiguous organizational relationships which prevailed, but there was a lack of general

[7] The Interboard Committee for Christian Work in Japan (office in New York) is the agent of eight foreign missions agencies desiring to cooperate in rendering assistance to the United Church of Christ in Japan and in such evangelistic, educational, social, medical, and other work among the people in Japan as may be mutually agreed upon.

agreement on how to solve the problems. Tommy sat through meeting after meeting and listened to arguments for and against the organizational unity of the church in Japan. Again and again she heard expositions of the passage on unity in John 17:20-23. "After one meeting I went home and looked in the Bible to see if these were the only verses in it," she commented.

It seemed to her that true unity, "oneness in Christ," already existed among Christians, and that this was a gift which men could no more create than they could earn salvation by their own efforts. This concept of the gift of unity placed the organizational forms of the church in a different perspective. The church, Tommy felt, was present in farmers' homes, in kindergarten opening exercises, at hospital bedsides, and in the earnest after-midnight conversation of two or three Christians.

In an effort to reach a working agreement with the United Church, the Shinsei Kai, in 1951, adopted two resolutions: (1) that the Shinsei Kai churches do not recognize the Nippon Kirisuto Kyodan (United Church of Japan) as a "church"; and (2) that the Nippon Kirisuto Kyodan be requested to give recognition to the Shinsei Kai as a Baptist denomination within the framework of the United Church. In 1952 these resolutions were rejected by the Kyodan General Assembly. Shortly thereafter, twelve Baptist congregations withdrew from the United Church and three newly-organized churches declined to enter the United Church.

The organizational tangle which resulted from these decisions was not unraveled until 1958 when the Baptist Domei, or Baptist Union, was formed by the Baptist churches outside of the United Church. In November, 1958, the boards recognized the Baptist Union and confirmed most of the actions taken in Japan. The Baptist Domei then applied for admission to the National Christian Council of Japan and to the Baptist World Alliance.

Speaking to the missionaries connected with the Shinsei Kai churches, Mr. B. L. Hinchman, field secretary of the American Baptist Mission, explained the Baptist interpretation of church unity:

> Baptists do not teach that they are the true church, the best church, or that they are a "church" at all. Rather, to be a member

of a local Baptist church is to be a member of the one and only true church, the Body of the Lord Jesus Christ. This concept of the church makes Baptists ecumenical by nature. All other Christians are brothers and sisters and no walls are recognized as dividing people into many so-called "churches." Faithfulness to the principles which we believe God has entrusted to us must never sever our fellowship with His sheep in other folds. Not only must we pray for these brethren and seek them out for fellowship, but we must take advantage of every opportunity of joining with them in projects of work demonstrating to the world that the church is one.

Spokesmen for the United Church affirm that the unity among Christians must be reflected in the church in the world:

As shown in the introduction and the first article of the Constitution, among the constituent bodies "each, while honoring each other their historic tenets, also enters into the fellowship of the holy catholic church." And this aim is not a remote goal to be held while firmly holding to one's own historic tenets. Regard for the special characteristics is recognized to be sure, but also it is said: "by the strange providence of God, in the unity given by His Spirit, we have come into the fellowship of the holy catholic church." This is where the emphasis is laid. Thus it is demanded that each one become conscious of its being a member of the universal church which is above the various parts, and any recognition of the historic differences of each must be within those limits.

Chapter Fourteen

BEGINNING IN JERUSALEM

As MORE MEMBERS WERE ADDED to the Kuji Church, the fellowship was faithful to its initial decision to witness to the countryside. Education and evangelism went hand in hand as small Sunday schools and meetings were held in nearby towns and villages. Christmas offered an opportunity for sharing the joys of the season, as well as its deeper meanings of worship and gratitude; and the founding of a branch center in the town of Karumai, forty miles from Kuji, made it possible to reach the people who lived in the mountains above the coast.

Going out two by two, church members conducted weekly Sunday schools. A young carpenter who had been one of the first graduates of the Kuji kindergarten became a Christian and persuaded his family to share his interest in Christian education. He and his parents opened their home on Saturday nights for "Sunday" school, and the attendance was soon over one hundred. One of the pupils described her experiences in the school:

> Supper is over and the clock says six. Some friends call me, and I go with them to our Saturday night school, singing all the way. It is very cold but we know our teachers will be there no matter what the weather is, and then, listening to a Bible story and singing the songs, my heart gets warm and I forget the cold. At first we were all together, little tiny tots and high school students, and we learned hymns and heard Bible stories and saw lovely pictures. But now we are separated, and we older ones have our own Bibles and are studying them. From Jesus' life I have learned more of kindness, and I want to serve him in my neighborhood. Kuji could be such a different place if we followed Jesus' teachings.

119

Education, of course, is not confined to the Sunday schools and the country meetings. It must go on in all phases of the program, even in the worship services. Programs and services in Japan often seem long to Americans, for few meetings last less than two hours, and gatherings of four or five hours are not uncommon. Tommy spoke to Takeshi, who had just delivered an unusually lengthy discourse, and asked him about the length of his sermons.

 I said to him, "Why do you preach so long every Sunday morning? In America ministers only speak for twenty minutes or half an hour." This was his answer, and I felt a little bit rebuked by it: "In America the pastors are talking to people who have a Christian background, and they know what the pastors are talking about; but here the people do not know what these things mean. I speak about God; but God to them is god with a little 'g,' and there are many of them; or I speak about love, but the only Japanese word for love is for sexual love; they do not understand the love of humanity. And so, when you have different connotations for the words, you have to do a lot of explaining. American ministers do not have to do that."

At Christmas time everyone is busy helping with the programs and services which celebrate the sacred festival. People who live in or near Kuji, the parents of the school children, adults who attend the cooking and sewing classes, and hospital patients come to the Christmas programs held at the Center. But Christmas also travels down the rocky coast and up the craggy mountains; Christmas comes to chilly school auditoriums, to barn-like town halls, and to smoke-darkened country homes.

 One of the postwar phenomena has been the almost universal celebration of Christmas. The outward trappings, the Christmas tree, the decorations, and the Christmas carols, are very popular. After the war it was not only the missionaries and the Japanese Christians, but the American military people who, by their generous gifts to worthy causes and their abundant good cheer, gave Japan something of the meaning of Christmas. In our far away isolated corner we, too, join the vast world family in celebrating the coming of the Prince of Peace. What a challenge, responsibility, and pleasure it is to be able to bring to people the beautiful story of Christmas for the very first time!

Kuni's deft hands and creative ideas are responsible for the

Christmas programs held at the Center for the kindergarten mothers, the Sunday school parents, and the adult education classes. It is she who plans the Nativity scene on the porch; and it is she who trains and costumes Mary and Joseph, the shepherds, the wise men, and the children from other lands who come offering gifts.

For the Christians in Kuji Christmas is not a family day, but a church day. It is a time for the individual Christians to gather together for worship, for the baptism of new members, and for Communion. The candlelight service, when newly baptized members are welcomed into the fellowship, is the climax of Christmas at Kuji. Kuni worked out an impressive service one year to dramatize the theme, "God Is Love." A light thrown on a cross made a large, effective shadow. To the music of Dvorak's "Largo" the church members marched slowly into the church, lighted their candles at the foot of the cross, and took their places to form the shape of the cross for the rest of the service.

But Christmas at Kuji is not limited to the Center nor confined to a single day. Throughout the month of December Tommy and Takeshi travel to the many villages which have invited them to come and hold a Christmas celebration, and they take along a portable Christmas tree. "We have it all fixed so that we can stand it up right away and decorate it, and the children's eyes nearly pop out as they see all those lovely decorations going on the little tree!" Using flannelgraph or the Japanese *kamishibai* (paper theater) they tell the Bible story, and they often show a Christmas film such as "Why the Littlest Camel Knelt." Sometimes they have two or three Christmases in one day, which becomes very tiring. The Japanese expect long programs, and even the most carefully planned schedule often proves impossible to keep.

 One time we were three hours late getting to a school. The station wagon was loaded with the Christmas tree and the decorations, with old Christmas cards and sacks of candy, and with the flannelgraph and the movie projector. The school principal and Mr. Yahaba and I were jammed in together with all of these things. Somehow, in all of that deep snow, we got a puncture and had to take everything out of the car. We stuck the tree in the snow for safekeeping, and Mr. Yahaba changed the tire. Then we put everything back, got in again, and rode about a mile. Suddenly someone exclaimed, "Where is the Christmas tree?" Well, the Christmas tree was sticking in the snow a mile back, and there was no way to turn around! Mr. Yahaba got out and ran back to get the little tree, and we put it in the car and went on. We were three hours late for that Christmas, but they were all waiting patiently for us.

School classrooms are heated in winter with wood-burning stoves, and those who sit near the stoves can keep fairly warm, but the auditoriums and gymnasiums where the programs are held have no heat. There are no chairs, so the children sit quietly on the floor throughout the programs. Tommy commented with a shiver, "I have learned many customs of this land, but never have I learned the gentle art of freezing gracefully; I just endure!"

From the first of December until New Year's Day the station wagon is loaded almost daily for its trek to the schools in the Ku-no-He area. Needles gradually disappear from the portable tree, and its decorations grow shabby from constant use. The snow lies deep, and the wind blows keen as Takeshi and Tommy make their way from village to village. School pianos accompany the piping voices of children singing their favorite Christmas hymn, "Silent Night, Holy Night."

 To our ears it is a complete disharmony, but I feel that there must be a higher harmony which is reaching the ears of heaven — the harmony of ultimate endeavor of doing one's best.

Late one snowy night after the program had ended, a peasant woman, a burden bearer of the land, insisted upon carrying much of the equipment on her own strong back and helping Tommy wade through the deep snow in the impenetrable darkness. The road was treacherous, and they held hands and tried to keep from falling in the freezing snow. As they parted, the woman took Tommy's hand in her own again and said softly, "I can never repay you for all you have done for us and for our children."

Karumai was the home of Miss Kamiiwa, the young school teacher who had come to Kuji during the war for help in facing the emotional problems which had overwhelmed her after the loss of her leg. She and her brother had been baptized and they attended the Kuji Church regularly, and soon they were looking for an opportunity to bring to their home village the knowledge of Christianity which had meant so much to them. Hoping to begin with the children, they came to the Kuji Center one day to suggest the opening of a kindergarten in Karumai.

Mr. Kamiiwa owned a building which he was willing to give for use as a kindergarten, but they needed financial help in remodeling it, and they needed training and guidance. As so often happened in Kuji work, here was an opportunity, but where could they find the money?

 We conferred with our pigs and told them to be fruitful and multiply because we needed the help that the sale of their off-spring would bring. They responded beautifully — one litter had fifteen in it, and through this and other ways we managed to make a very lovely building out of an old house.

Miss Kamiiwa and another young teacher lived at the Kuji Center for a year, working in the kindergarten and participating in all of the Center activities. When the branch center was opened, it followed the Kuji pattern. Soon there were seventy children in the Karumai kindergarten, there was a flourishing Sunday school, and there were meetings for interested adults. The work there has been a very satisfying thing with twelve persons baptized into the Kuji Church and attending its services. It is a long way to come, but the Karumai people come to church nearly every Sunday.

The gospel message is not always preached in words; often it is demonstrated in lives that suggest humbly and simply what the message means in Jerusalem, and in Kuji, and among all nations of the world.

Chapter Fifteen

A HOSPITAL FOR MRS. ASANAI

THE SOUND OF THE RINGING TELEPHONE at the Center shattered the silence of the winter night, and the man who rolled out of his warm bed to answer it guessed that someone was in trouble. He was right; over the wire came the frantic voice of Mr. Asanai, explaining that his wife was sick, terribly sick. She was hemorrhaging, and he did not believe that she could live long, let alone bear the child she was expecting. He knew how bad the weather was and that the road might be impassable, but could the doctor come; would he try to come?

Mr. Asanai was one of a group of settlers in the village of Iyasaka, men who had settled on mountain land and were struggling to make a living there. They had come to the north after the war and had suffered many hardships as they tried to farm the unproductive land. Iyasaka is a mile off the main road, and the connecting road is usually impassable in winter.

When the station wagon reached the branch road, Mr. Asanai was waiting there, for the station wagon could go no farther. The men started down the road on foot, carrying the stretcher and their medical equipment, and it was after midnight when they reached the Asanai home. The doctor brushed the snow off his coat and knelt beside Mrs. Asanai. It was evident that she was seriously ill and in need of immediate hospitalization and blood plasma if she were to live. Her eyes, wide with pain and fear, flooded with gratitude when she realized that help had come. The stretcher was quickly prepared, and Mr. Asanai and the men from the Center started to carry it back to the main

124

road. The storm had grown worse, and the mile to the road seemed an interminable distance; but two lives were at stake, and so the men hurried on.

When they reached the hospital, lights were bright in the operating room, and soon the patient was receiving life-giving plasma. While the doctor cared for the patient, several of the men joined Mr. Asanai in the waiting room. Cups of hot tea helped to warm them after their wintry ordeal, and words of comfort and hope helped to calm and encourage the frightened husband. The waiting was not easy, but it was not long before they learned that Mrs. Asanai would live. And live she did, to bear a healthy child and to return to Iyasaka to share the life of her pioneering husband!

Shortly after World War II ended, an idealistic Red Cross doctor from Morioka had visited Kuji. He understood the country people and felt a deep concern for their health after years of struggle and deprivation. At first he approached the political authorities in Kuji and nearby towns, seeking to interest them in sponsoring a clinic, but they were not in sympathy with his ideas and resented the suggestions which he made. As a last resort, Dr. Kinoshita went to talk to Takeshi Yahaba. Here he found a sympathetic listener, a man who shared his concern for the health of the people. Takeshi offered the Center building for use as a clinic and agreed to entertain the doctors who would come to hold the clinic every two weeks. "We were delighted, the Red Cross was delighted, and the people were even more delighted. They hadn't had any medical attention for at least five years," Takeshi recalls.

Until the immediate medical emergency had been met, the Red Cross doctors came regularly to Kuji and cared for their patients in one of the kindergarten rooms. Thereafter they came as contract surgeons, and a few bed patients were cared for in an old Japanese house beside the Center building. Remembering how he had felt when he could not find a doctor willing to come to his sick wife and child, Takeshi began to think about opening a hospital and operating it on Christian principles of care and concern for each individual patient. He knew that Iwate Ken had the highest infant mortality rate in Japan, for there was no obstetrician in the county; the women know nothing about proper diet, and they often worked in the cold water of the rice paddies until the last minute before delivery.

To open any new work required both money and land, and so Tommy appealed to those who believed in Kuji; then she borrowed money and finally raised enough to start plans for a hospital building, but land was secured only after months of lengthy negotiations. "Why does it take so much time to get anything done? Everything demands much, much time, and much, much unwinding of red tape. Patience is *not* one of my virtues — but of course, I have all of the others!" At last the building was begun, and the clinic rooms, the pharmacy, the operating room, and the wards began to take shape. Equipment was installed, and the hospital was nearly ready for service. To the other problems was added the almost insuperable difficulty of obtaining a medical staff. Competent doctors, sympathetic to the Kuji ideals, were hard to find. Patiently Takeshi and Kuni scoured Japan for doctors and nurses who were willing to face the hardships of life in the country, and by 1959 the Kuji hospital was equipped and staffed to serve the community.

The practice of medicine in Japan has reflected the three-way struggle between Japanese, Chinese, and western thought which characterizes Japanese history in every field. Elements of Japanese and Chinese medical techniques and superstitions have persisted into the scientific present, particularly in rural areas.

Japanese medical practice originated in the misty age of the demi-gods sometime before the Christian era, and the first knowledge of the cure of disease is attributed to the teachings of the two of their deities. Tradition asserts that early researchers experimented with monkeys to determine the reaction of the animals to various vegetable substances. Records of longevity were also kept, and it was solemnly noted that few people lived beyond the age of one hundred years.

An often-repeated legend tells of the coming of the first Chinese physician. Desiring to escape the tyranny of a certain government, the physician explained to the Emperor that he wished to leave China to seek out the medicine of immortality. "This," he assured the Emperor, "is a plant which grows only in Japan, and the plant is so sensitive and tender that it will yield its virtues only when handled by virtuous hands." Intrigued by the story, the Emperor permitted the physician and his party to leave China and set sail for Japan. The clever physician arrived at the Japanese Imperial Court where he introduced Chinese medical techniques. In time a temple was erected in his honor, "for having introduced good manners and useful knowledge."

The introduction of Buddhism in the sixth century had a pronounced effect on medicine. Buddhist priests served as physicians and medical instructors, and a medical school was founded which taught the Chinese system of internal medicine and the cultivation of medicinal plants. But a plague broke out in A.D. 806, and the advocates of "Japanese medical art as taught in ancient times by men and gods" urged the Emperor to prohibit Chinese medicine. The age of borrowing was coming to an end, and the nationalist faction in Japan condemned everything Chinese and urged a revival of native culture.

Nagata Tokuhon (1512-1630) was one of the great practitioners of natural, or Japanese, medicine. He sought to work with nature, and he believed that the body's demands would suggest to the alert physician what treatment he should prescribe. When a nobleman came to Tokuhon suffering with a fever, the physician asked him what he liked and what he disliked. "I would like to remove my clothing and have the screens taken from my room so I can feel the breezes. Then I would like to eat some watermelon and have all of the cold water I can drink." Tokuhon prescribed the things desired by the man and cured his fever. He was a clever psychologist who sought to learn the cause of a patient's worries before he treated nervous disorders. Once he understood the patient's problem, by encouragement, by exciting anger or sorrow, or even by inflicting physical pain, he aroused his patients to health.

Francis Xavier reached Japan in 1549, and he brought with him some knowledge of European medicine. Luis de Almedeida, a lay brother of the Jesuit order, founded a hospital in Kyoto as well as other charitable institutions. Two medical priests were in charge of a dispensary for the poor and cultivated a large garden where they grew medicinal plants. But after the Jesuits were driven from Japan and foreign books were forbidden, actual medical knowledge was minimized. Oriental ideas of harmony and pantheistic emphases on nature's laws again became dominant, and philosophy rather than science provided the basis for medical practice.

After 1621 the Japanese were forbidden to have any contact with foreigners, but the little company of Dutch traders on the island of Deshima always included a physician, and Japanese doctors managed to communicate with them and to learn of European medical techniques.

In 1771 a courageous Japanese physician named Gempaku Sugita obtained two Dutch anatomical books. As he read them, he realized that their illustrations varied from the ones he had studied in Chinese texts. He obtained permission to dissect the body of an executed criminal, and from this experiment he learned that the Dutch books were correct. Joined by two scholarly companions, he began to study the Dutch language and the Dutch textbooks, and four years later the three men published their *New Treatise on Anatomy* in Japanese.

The Chinese school of medicine did not die out, but it maintained its influential position at the Court and continued to send petitions to the Emperor, protesting the study of western medicine for internal disease. Europeans and Asiatics, insisted the Chinese scholars, were dissimilar in their nature.

The government settled the controversy among the three schools of medicine by publishing an edict, in 1875, which stated that the examinations for medical licenses would be in western medicine only. Many Japanese studied abroad in Europe and in the United States, and then they returned to Japan as trained specialists who have made outstanding contributions.

Despite the official recognition and acceptance of western medical science, many traditional practices of doubtful medical value were common. Practitioners of acapuncture continued to slip slender needles into their patients, and believers in moxa continued to burn tiny pyramids of powdered grass upon the skin of the sick. The poor and the ignorant were often victimized by unscrupulous quacks, or they pauperized themselves by buying offerings to healing deities.

In the decades of the 1920's and the 1930's there was steady progress in the medical profession, although the death rate remained high by western standards. This progress was disrupted by World War II.

War damage was severe, for hospitals, medical schools, and pharmacies were destroyed in the cities which burned in the wake of allied bombers. Most of the population was tired and hungry and had little resistance to disease. The burden of military and civilian casualties at the end of World War II was almost beyond the resources of the Japanese medical profession. Takeshi's simple statement about the town of Kuji at that time is eloquent of its condition: "The people had had no medical care for five years."

Even though the 1950's brought great improvements in the ratio of doctors, nurses, and hospitals to the population of the nation as a whole, most of the medical facilities were concentrated in the cities. The farmer doubled up with appendicitis and the fisherman whose head was cracked by a boom had small chance of reaching a doctor or a hospital in a hurry. Their pregnant wives were still delivered by midwives in homes that were far from sanitary, and the infant death rate and the mortality rate among mothers in the country remained well above that of their urban contemporaries.

The Kuji Christian Hospital, opened in 1959, played its part in caring for the people in Ku-no-He County. A steady stream of patients came to the out-patient clinic where a general practitioner, an obstetrician, and an ophthalmologist were on duty. In the modern operating room a surgeon worked to care for the surgical patients, and a well-trained corps of nurses cared for the forty bed patients in the wards. The presence of an ophthalmologist on the staff led to a decline in the high rate of optical diseases and blindness in the area. For years farmers who worked in the rice paddies had suffered from the stings of insects in their eyes. If these bites were not treated, an eye infection usually developed, and all too often the patient was blinded. Now the relatively simple treatment was close at hand, and the rate of infection was curbed.

Japanese hospital patients are traditionally accompanied by

friends or relatives who do the nursing and cook their meals. In the Kuji Hospital the meals are prepared in a central kitchen under the direction of a trained dietician and served on bright, brass-colored trays. A good Japanese meal should be as pleasant to see as it is to taste, and the bowls of rice, pickles, vegetables, and fish are arranged in a colorful and appealing fashion. The elimination of individual cooking fires helps to keep the hospital clean and bright. Visiting rules are not enforced with the same strictness that is often imposed in American hospitals, and friends and relatives are free to come and go at will, unless some restriction is necessary for the patient's welfare. Children and old people, both of whom find hospitalization frightening, are comforted by the presence of relatives at their bedsides.

The healing witness was not bound by the township limits; doctors and nurses went into isolated mountain villages to hold clinics for those too poor to afford the trip to Kuji. In Kosode the clinic was set up in a small building next to a pig pen, and Tommy was given the job of killing flies while the doctor and nurse worked. A loudspeaker set up on the mountain announced the opening of the clinic, and soon patients began to come. Women, carrying their children, came from the fields, and men came from the forests. Once a talkative eighty-year-old grandmother told of the birth of her own children without benefit of doctor or midwife, and she announced proudly that she had sixty grandchildren and great-grandchildren. Swatting another cluster of persistent flies, Tommy reflected on the squalor of the town and the sturdiness of the farm people: "A doctor once told me that a *lot* of dirt is safe, but a *little* dirt is dangerous; according to that, people in this village are perfectly safe!"

Each year at Christmas Tommy and Takeshi present programs at schools and community halls in many of the villages of the Ku-no-He area. One of their stops is the home of Mrs. Asanai about a mile from the main road in the little village of Iyasaka. Each year Mrs. Asanai serves tea after the program, and as she looks at the child asleep on his futon, she remembers with gratitude a doctor who came to her on a stormy winter night from the Center at Kuji.

Chapter Sixteen

 A SCHOOL FOR SHIGE CHAN

ON THE DAY when the first atomic bomb blasted the city of Hiroshima into eternity, Shige Chan and her mother were away; they had gone out into the country to bargain for vegetables from the August harvest, and so they escaped the blast and the ensuing dangers of radiation. But the father of Shige Chan was a city official of Hiroshima, and he was at work in his office. His wife hurried through the dying city, and found her husband alive but badly burned. Then, moving through the nightmare, she took him from the ruins and, for the few days that he lived, she nursed him as best she could. Then, since she was a native of Iwate Ken, she made the long, difficult journey back north, and somehow, despite the blasted railroads and the turmoil that marked the end of the war, she managed to reach Kuji. She and Shige Chan were safe!

To Kuni and Takeshi the Kuji Kindergarten had been their deed to Anathoth, and they had kept the kindergarten open throughout the war years no matter what difficulties they had to face. The little children who came to the kindergarten when it was started in 1938 were often ragged and dirty, and sometimes they were hungry; but the postwar children who filed into the same room were the victims of five years of concentrated misery.

United in their concern for the hungry little children, Japanese government officials and occupation authorities worked together to establish a school lunch program, and they drew food from any source which had a supply of needed nourishment. Japanese military rations were released to the school lunch program at first, and later surplus dried milk and wheat from abroad made it possible to continue to provide each child with a lunch of 300 to 600 calories. Mother's clubs and teachers somehow rounded up the necessary kitchen equipment and did the work of preparing and serving the food. Food from agencies with complicated alphabetical titles flowed into the rice bowls of seven and a half million children in Japan.

Among the boys and girls who licked their bowls clean of the last drop of milk and picked up the last tiny crumb of bread was Shige Chan, child of Hiroshima, for compassionate officialdom and compassionate individuals united to see that Shige Chan was fed and clothed. But man does not live by bread alone, and she found a joy that helped to wipe out the memories of her wartime terror; she attended the kindergarten at Kuji. However, these years soon passed, and Shige Chan, along with the other children, found her way into the schools that would in a large measure affect the future mindset of her generation. What sort of schools were Shige Chan and her tiny contemporaries to attend? What philosophy was to direct their government? What goals were to be set for their future?

In early Japan, education was limited to the upper classes, for their pattern of education borrowed from China came to be identified with the Court and to be called *daigaku*, or great learning. Provincial governors established clan schools, and influential families established private family schools which were designated as *kokugaku*, or national learning. The Buddhist temples educated their novices and established temple schools where a few of the common people learned such practical disciplines as reading, letter-writing, arithmetic, etiquette, and calligraphy.

Under the Japanese brand of Confucianism which prevailed during the Tokugawa period, teachers and scholars were held in high respect, and students were expected to be diligent. On the desk of many a Japanese school child stands the figure of a sturdy little boy carrying a bundle of faggots on his back and reading a book. His was the kind of success story that the Japanese love to tell their children.

Sontoku Ninomiya was born in Odawara, a coastal town near Tokyo, during the late eighteenth century. When he was twelve, the Sakawa River overflowed and ruined his family's farm land, and Sontoku saw the suffering which the flood of salty tidal water brought to his village. He vowed that when he grew up he would learn how to help villages that had been blighted in this tragic fashion. But more troubles were in store for the boy, for he was left an orphan and had to work very hard. He could no longer attend school, so he tried to make up for his lack of opportunity by reading his books as he carried wood from the mountains to sell to his neighbors. He lived with a miserly uncle who refused to let him have any oil for light to read in the evening, but, undaunted, Sontoku sowed rape-seeds in a little plot of unclaimed land, and, thus, he obtained oil so that he could study at night.

Hattori Jurobei, one of the clan ministers, was impressed by the studious and hardworking Sontoku and employed him to care for his three sons. Sontoku accompanied the three boys to school, and, while they studied inside the classroom, he stood outside listening and learning the lessons. Eventually he was placed in charge of the clan finances, which were in a deplorable condition. Sontoku laid down three rules for the clansmen: Only rice and soup were to be served at each meal; only cotton clothing was to be worn; and there were to be no frivolous expenditures. In three years he put the clan on a sound financial footing.

His life from then on was one long success story. Sontoku had not forgotten his boyhood dream of helping villages in times of natural disaster, and he became an expert in reclamation and rehabilitation work. As a climax to his career he was employed by the Tokugawa government for extensive engineering projects. After his death a shrine was erected to his memory in Odawara, and an association of his disciples carried on his work.

The shock of contact with western nations which followed the opening of the country after 1854 profoundly affected Japanese education. Astute Japanese leaders realized that universal education was a vital asset to the country and an important instrument of national policy. Through the schools they could unite the nation, teach it to revere the Emperor, and make it strong enough to resist the foreigners.

When Arinori Mori became Minister of State for Education,

in 1885, he launched an ambitious school system that eventually reached throughout the nation and gave the Japanese the distinction of having the world's highest literacy rate. Mori had served as Japanese envoy in Washington, and while he was there, he became interested in the American public school system. He enlisted the aid of Dr. David Murray, Professor at Rutgers College, to help him establish the Japanese school system. Under Mori's leadership thousands of school buildings went up, and thousands of teachers were trained and sent forth to teach millions of Japanese children to read and write.

The school system reflected the spirit of the guiding educational ordinance which stated: "In the administration of all schools, it must be kept in mind, what is done is not done for the sake of the pupils, but for the sake of the country." The Imperial Rescript on Education issued in 1890 became the creed of the nation. Although Japanese children sat at desks instead of kneeling on the tatami, and discarded kimonos for western uniforms, the emphasis on moral training and national loyalty expressed in the Imperial Rescript was fundamental to the whole system of national education.

At last even women breached the Confucian barrier which had separated them from their brothers' intellectual pursuits, but much of their progress they owed to the Christian missionaries. The wife of one of the earliest missionaries, Mrs. James Curtis Hepburn, held classes in her home for young ladies, and the first girls' school in Japan, Ferris School in Yokohama, was a mission school. By 1900 the Japanese government cautiously conceded that women might benefit from higher education and built the first national women's university. Citing the scattered but notable contributions of Japan's women scholars and authors, the president of the newly-founded Nippon Women's University declared cautiously that these cases justified the conclusion that women could pursue higher learning and still retain their traditional feminine virtues.

The climate of liberalism which influenced Japan immediately after the first World War was most evident in the academic world. John Dewey, American educational philosopher and father of progressive education, lectured at Waseda University

in 1918 and at Tokyo Imperial University in 1919. On his return
to the United States he reported that he could feel the breath
of liberalism in Japan where he had felt none before.[8]

But a reaction was coming. The Japanese Exclusion Act of
1924 did much to disillusion and offend the liberal and democratic thinkers of Japan. Conservative elements feared the
radical interest of the students in socialism and communism, and
sought to curb this trend by limiting academic freedom. In 1925
the first thought control bill was passed, and from then on there
was increasing pressure on the schools. The thought controllers
gained almost complete command of the schools in the 1930's,
and in 1933 they declared that all things not in conformity with
national policy must be excluded from Japanese thinking. University professors were chosen for their loyalty to Japanese
tradition rather than for their ability, and throughout the school
system the Japanese spirit and imperial reverence were stressed.
Alas for the high hopes of the Meiji educators, the philosophy of
education for the benefit of the state had produced a school
system in which "Loyalty and patriotism were considered the
highest virtues; individualism, internationalism, and pacificism
were allied with treason."[9]

As she ate her roll and drank her milk and played with her
sandpile classmates, Shige Chan knew little of such words as
nationalism, democracy, and liberalism, and they meant nothing
to her; nevertheless, Japanese and American educators were
busy planning for her education.

The United States Education Mission to Japan, a committee
of twenty-seven American educators, arrived in Japan in 1946.
On their arrival they met and worked with a group of educational
leaders who faced a school system that was physically shattered;
its buildings had burned in the holocaust of war, its students
were undernourished and poorly prepared, and its textbooks had
been mutilated to remove objectionable nationalistic material.

[8] John Dewey, "Public Opinion in Japan," *The New Republic*, 28: Supplement 15-18, November 16, 1921.

[9] Ronald S. Anderson, *Japan: Three Epochs of Modern Education*, Bul-
letin No. 11, U. S. Department of Health, Education and Welfare.
Washington, D. C.: U. S. Government Printing Office, 1959, p. 19.

Despite the obstacles, the educators promptly decided to extend the existing six-year program of free compulsory education to nine years. With some help from the national government, the local communities somehow managed to provide and staff 76,000 new classrooms. As high school and university education was broadened and coeducation was encouraged, efforts were made to decentralize education and to encourage local boards to take over some of the responsibilities of running the school system. *Shushin,* the training in moral and spiritual principles which had occupied a large part of the prewar curriculum, was dropped to be replaced by social studies, a broad combination of the material previously covered in history, geography, and moral philosophy.

Although they benefited from many of these reforms, rural children remained at a disadvantage in the postwar period, just as they had in the earlier years. Many of them still hiked for miles through the mountains to study in forlorn and cheerless schools, and very few had the opportunities for higher education that urban children enjoyed.

A report issued shortly after 1949 noted that Iwate Ken stood at the bottom of the list in education, and the investigators added that the poverty-stricken northern area was at least sixty years behind Tokyo. Commented Tommy, "We could have told them that and saved them the trouble, only I should have been tempted to say one hundred years."

The success of the Kuji kindergarten, where hundreds of children spent two or three preschool years, led to a demand for an elementary school. However, the problems to be faced in opening such a school were many.

 Could we get children to come to the primary school? Would the parents see the advantages of a small private school? We knew that we couldn't charge very much tuition, and that the school would always be in the red, but it seemed to us that it might be the most effective way in which we could work and train leaders for the future. After much debate and much unwinding of red tape, we started a little primary school in 1952.

But "starting a little primary school" meant a great deal more than merely welcoming five small Japanese citizens into the first grade. Under Japanese law a private school must maintain a complete school system through all of the nine years of compulsory education. Securing competent teachers was a continuing problem, for qualified teachers were in demand to teach in the national schools, and qualified teachers with a Christian background were particularly hard to locate. Few teachers wished to live and teach in the country or in an isolated town without entertainment facilities or intellectual stimulation. The supply of dedication needed for the work was not always equal to the demand. But somehow Tommy and the Yahabas secured qualified teachers with the needed Christian dedication for their task and the Homare (Praise) School at Kuji was born.

The Homare School is one of the few Protestant Christian elementary schools in Japan. Although some 125,000 students are enrolled in schools connected with the Christian Education Association, most of them are in high schools and colleges; only a few thousand attend Christian primary schools. Six years after the opening of the elementary school at Kuji the middle school was started, for the first graders who had attended the original class were now ready for the seventh grade.

 Education in Japan has not been conducive to thinking. To quote from a recent Japanese magazine article, "The Japanese, especially those who have traveled abroad, now often comment on the lack of emphasis on logic in Japanese business and education. The quickest way to paralyze a classroom of Japanese students is to ask a question stressing reasoning." We are trying to overcome this in our own small way.

Chapter Seventeen

A FARM FOR SKEPTICS

There are the roads always narrow and mostly at the wood's edge or the river's.

There is the straw piled on brushwood bridges off the loam and the trees only growing at the god's house, never in the fields.

There are the whole plains empty of roofs, squared into flats of water, no inch for walking but the dike backs, not so much as a green weed at the foot of the telegraph poles or a corner patch gone wild.

There are the fields empty of crows after harvest: thin picking for black wings after cloth ones.

There are the men under moonlight in the mountain villages breaking the winter snowdrifts on the paddies to save days of spring.

There are the forest floors swept clean and the sweepings bundled into careful, valuable piles.

There are the houses without dogs, the farms without grass-eating cattle. . . .[10]

TOO MANY MEN ON TOO LITTLE LAND; this has been the classic dilemma of Japan. So much of the country is mountainous that only about twenty percent can be cultivated; therefore the fields and the paddies must be farmed intensively. Human labor is recklessly expended, for over six hundred man-hours a year go into the production of an acre of wheat and over eight hundred man-hours into the production of an acre of rice. Double cropping is common. After the grain crops have been harvested, the fields are cultivated and planted with vegetables, and quantities of organic and chemical fertilizer are used on the plants.

---

[10] "Of Many Men on Little Land," *Fortune Magazine*, September, 1936.

138

Despite the handicaps imposed by nature, Japanese farmers have by hard work and efficient farming practices produced yields as high as three tons of rice to the acre in favorable southern paddies.

But in the Kuji area the climate is too severe and the season too short for double cropping, and the soil is among the poorest on earth. Subsistence farming was the rule rather than the exception. As early as 1935 Dr. Toyohiko Kagawa had bluntly pointed out the trouble with northern farmers, in these words: "They are still trying to raise southern crops in a northern climate."

The idea of starting a farm to demonstrate and teach dairying grew slowly in Takeshi's mind. It originated with a garbage collection route which he started in 1948. His financial resources were almost non-existent at that time, yet he wanted very much to hold a Farmers' Gospel School for the young men of the nearby villages. He bought two pigs with a little money he had saved, and he arranged to collect the garbage from three of the houses in Kuji to feed the pigs. Each morning, before the six o'clock prayer meeting, he made his rounds. He emptied the garbage pails and then cleaned them out with a brush. Soon two more families were added to his route, and eventually he was collecting garbage from fifty houses; the pigs were thriving.

> I had no gloves, and my hands stuck to the iron of the cart that I used, sometimes causing the skin to come off, but I was happy. I knew that by selling some of the offspring of these pigs, we could finance the Farmers' Gospel School.

Twenty-eight men came to the first school to share in the Christian fellowship and to learn something of improved farming techniques. Next year another school was held, and professors came from the State Agricultural Department in Morioka to speak on agricultural problems. "From the worship service at six in the morning until the end of the play hour at nine-thirty at night, we tried to demonstrate Christian living and working together." Farmers who attended the schools began to see the value of agricultural education, but they were not convinced that much progress was possible in their district.

On the outskirts of Kuji, land had been set aside for a government demonstration farm, but lack of heavy farm machinery, livestock, capital, and experienced leadership had handicapped its development. The farsighted postwar governor of Iwate Prefecture, Mr. Kenkichi Kokubun, understood the condition of the farmers in the prefecture, and he was interested in any innovations that might improve their standard of living. His concern for the farmers won him the title of "The Country Governor." During his tenure, negotiations for a possible lease of the demonstration farm began between the Center and the government. Since he was familiar with the work at Kuji and had a high respect for the reliability of the Center leadership, Mr. Kokubun did all that he could to further the proposal.

After his death his successor, Mr. Senichi Abe, also regarded the plan with favor, commenting, "If Thomasine Allen says she will do it, then she will do it. We can trust her." Negotiations were finally completed, and the government turned over 125 acres of scrubby hill land to the Kuji Center for use as a demonstration farm and an agricultural school. When Takeshi assured the governor that he hoped to make the desert land "blossom as a rose," the governor replied in an equally biblical vein that he hoped to see it become "a land flowing with milk and honey."

To have the land was one thing, but to make it productive was something else again. The neighbors had little faith in the project. Settlers on nearby plots watched day laborers clearing the area of scrub timber and underbrush, and they shook their heads, for they knew all too well that the chances of making that land grow anything at all were slim. They had seen the government workers struggling to clear the farm, and they had seen them give up and leave. When Takeshi talked of his plans and hopes for the future, they shook their heads knowingly and assured him, "You'll run away just like all of the others did."

A successful and prosperous dairy industry had grown up on the island of Hokkaido, and the Christian Dairy Farming School at Sapporo had pioneered in training farmers in dairy agriculture through its classrooms as well as its widespread extension work. Several professors from the school came to study the land and the climate near Kuji and to determine whether dairying could be successfully established in the area. They assured Takeshi that the land and the climate indicated that dairy cattle could prosper in Ku-no-He County. Consultation continued between the Center and the Christian Dairy Farming School, and eventually several graduates came as staff members to teach agriculture and dairying at Kuji.

The steps of reclamation were now clear: The land must be cleared and broken, the soil tested and restored; stock must be obtained, and feed for the stock must be assured. Tommy's faith and interest had long since outrun her financial resources. They needed so many things — buildings, farm equipment, and livestock. "But the means were marvelously supplied in many ways," she says.

Two close friends from America were on their way to the Baptist World Alliance meeting in London, and they came to Kuji. During their visit Tommy learned that there was a chance of securing some heifers through Heifer Project and Church World Service. Her guest telephoned Tokyo at once and made arrangements for four Jersey heifers to be sent to Kuji on the next shipment. Although the heifers were a gift, the recipient had to pay the transportation, so church groups and friends raised money for the shipping costs. It was a big day when the cattle finally arrived in Kuji and were settled in stalls built at the Center.

Work was soon started at the farm itself, but clearing the land proved slow going. American friends were able to help again by sending a tractor, and at last it was possible to put the land under cultivation; soon the fields sprouted with corn, alfalfa, and pasture grasses. The pigs continued to be fruitful and multiplied, bringing a much needed income to the project, and soon it was possible to build a barn and silo and to buy more dairy cattle. With government help and encouragement, a school building was constructed and a two-year course in vocational agriculture was started.

According to the eighth-century chronicle, the *Nihongi*, the first mention of dairy or meat products is found in the tale of Ukemochi-no-Kami who was put to death by order of the Sun Goddess, Amaterasu, for the crime of keeping cattle and using animal products for food. However, historical references tell of the occasional use of milk as a medicine. During the Asuka Period a Japanese expeditionary force to Korea brought a Chinese named Chiso to Japan. His son, Yona, presented cow's milk to the Emperor Kotoku, and as a reward he was named Yamato Kusuri-no-Omi, or, Official Pharmacist of Yamato Province, and his special appointment was "Director of Cow's Milk." The tenth-century records of the Court Physician indicate that a supply of milk was furnished to the Imperial Court.

Traditionally vegetarian, the Buddhist hierarchy engaged in a heated controversy concerning the propriety of drinking milk. According to the pro-milk faction, Gautama Buddha himself found that drinking milk refreshed him and made him strong and well. The Onin Wars of the fifteenth century disrupted the dairy business, and there is no reference to milk or herds until 1728, when the enlightened Shogun Yoshimune imported three white cows from Holland and established a farm near Chiba for producing cheese. Just as in earlier days when milk had been consumed for its medicinal value, the Shogun's cheese was valued for its therapeutic effect.

One of the upsetting demands made by Commodore Perry was his request for beef to supply his crew with fresh meat, but the only cattle in nineteenth-century Japan were draft animals, referred to as "human beasts." It had never occurred to the Japanese to eat them. Shortly thereafter a British ship called at the port of Hakodate with the same request, "Would the Japanese please supply fresh meat for the crew?" Shocked authorities finally suggested that the British raise and butcher their own stock on a farm which the government would make available to them for that purpose.

In later years resident foreigners paid dearly for the meat and dairy products to which they were accustomed. Townsend Harris, the first American consul to Japan, paid the price of a bale of rice for one *go*, less than one-third of a pint, of milk. As foreigners became more numerous in the 1860's and 1870's, they brought condensed milk in tins, and eventually they imported milch cows. A young man named Tomekichi Maeda, who had learned from the Dutch to milk cows, opened a milk store in 1863 in Ota-machi, Yokohama. He is supposed to have undertaken this daring venture because he was impressed by the height and build of the foreigners.

The Meiji Government encouraged the breeding of both milch cows and beef cattle, but Buddhist priests, traditionally vegetarian, objected strenuously; the government met their objections by proclaiming, in 1872, that the priests could eat meat. Progressive and liberal leaders such as Yukichi Fukazawa, founder of Keio University, urged the eating of meat with the same ardor with which they urged the adoption of political and educational innovations.

However, this new legislation was not always acceptable to the people; on the day when the first meat was prepared and served in the more conservative and devout homes, grandmothers carefully sealed up the doors of the Butsudan, the Buddhist household shrine, in order that the ancestors might not be affronted by the breaking of the old dietary customs. These customs were as much social as they were religious, for the poorer people and the lower classes ate meat — not beef, but game; and Japan's most famous dish, sukiyaki, traditionally originated when game was grilled by hunters on the blade of a shovel. Rude customs and coarse foods were abhorrent to the socially elect classes, and few who were grandmothers in the Meiji period ever changed their menus. Whenever meat was served, they ate alone and apart from the family in silent disapproval.

In postwar Japan most of the historical prejudices against milk and meat have disappeared. Today shoppers dropping into department store dining rooms for lunch examine a window full of samples of the appetizing dishes available, and the wide variety displayed indicates changing tastes. Traditional Japanese foods such as fish, rice, pickles and vegetables are there, to be sure, but so are salads and fruits, cutlets and spaghetti, milk and ice cream. In the basement delicatessens of the department stores, city housewives buy butter, cheese, meat, vegetables, and a wide variety of canned and frozen foods. The Japanese now eat twice as much fruit as they did before the war, enjoying golden tangerines, crisp winter pears, and giant strawberries. And they eat more than twice as much protein; eggs, chicken, beef, and pork are increasingly popular.

But the biggest change in the Japanese diet is the three hundred percent increase in the consumption of dairy products. Industrial plants serve milk in lunchrooms, schools include it in school lunch programs, and railroad stations sell bottles of milk warmed in steam tables. Ice cream is sold by vendors at theaters, on trains, and in restaurants and coffee houses. *Aisu Kurimu* (ice cream) has been added to the list of Japanicized English words which make up a fascinating fragment of the colloquial language.

These changes assured the Kuji planners that dairy products would find a ready market. On the demonstration farm, scrub vegetation and stubborn roots yielded to plow and harrow; and, before many years had passed, rows of corn tasseled in the fields, and pasture grasses turned the barren slopes into meadows. A herd of cattle grazed contentedly on the green hillside and meandered back to a sturdy, modern barn at sundown. In a pleasant dark red school building a handful of young farmers lived and studied together the techniques of scientific dairying and agriculture which Takeshi had laboriously mastered during the war. But the primary goals of the Kuji Christian Center were neither agricultural success nor nutritional improvement, although these ends were most important and highly desirable.

What did the skeptical neighbors think, those who had predicted an early failure for the whole project? As they watched its growth and development over the years, even the doubting "Tamashiis" from the nearby farms were convinced that the farm was now a reality. Eventually a little delegation came to see Takeshi and to ask him for some help:

> We've watched you people and seen you stick to it. You didn't run away, and you've made more progress in three years than we thought was possible in five or ten. We think it is because of Christianity. Would one of your Christian teachers from the farm come to us and open a Sunday school for our children?

Chapter Eighteen

FOUR IS A VERY LARGE NUMBER

SEPTEMBER IN KUJI IS A PLEASANT MONTH; the rice fields are heavy with grain ripe for harvest, vegetables and fruits are abundant, and the sun shines benevolently on the checkered fields and the wooded mountains. Scarlet and gold leaves flash among the deep green of the pine trees and the worn grey of the rocks. The gorge that leads to the village of Kawai unrolls before the eye of the traveler like an autumn landscape scroll by Sesshu.

But September is also typhoon season, and, with the approach of fall, weather maps begin to show the build-up of tropical storms which move northward.

Several months after her retirement, Tommy was preparing to celebrate her birthday, and several friends from the Baptist mission were coming to spend the weekend with her. She planned the dinner carefully; there would be canned ham and sweet potatoes, fresh coffee cake, and, of course, a birthday cake.

Then up from the far reaches of the South Pacific came the storm. As it swept across the islands of Japan, its high winds left destruction in their wake, and its torrential rains left floods. Over Kuji, clouds obscured the sun, and the wind began to blow an unusually fierce gust even for a country accustomed to gales. Soon rain was lashing the trees, flattening the heavy rice plants into the mud, and driving through the wooden shutters of the buildings. An eerie, supernatural darkness descended over the town, and the placid little river began to rise. But the Japanese are accustomed to severe storms and to typhoons, and they do not panic easily. Although the town had had its natural and man-

145

made disasters, it lay outside of the usual storm track; and moreover it had never had a flood. This time, however, the rain poured steadily down on the mountains and turned the gentle stream into a raging torrent. Finally the river topped its banks!

Sirens blew to signal evacuation of the town, and Tommy and the others started across the flooded fields and the slippery dikes toward the safety of the hills. After only a few steps they realized that they had waited too long; the water was too deep to ford. It was impossible now to cross the low paddy land that lay between them and safety; indeed, it was almost out of the question to walk through the swirling water at all. They turned back and retreated to Tommy's home to seek safety on the second floor, hoping that the house would survive the storm and that they would be safe there. Flood waters surged through the lower floor of the house and swamped it completely; then they rose past the first step, the second, and the third. Tommy watched as the water climbed step by step. Finally it stopped and began to recede; all of the people were safe, and the house still stood. But the flood waters had left behind tons of muck and mud and had done thousands of dollars worth of damage.

 I am now sitting in the midst of the debris, thinking of how many times during my long years in Iwate I have done relief work through famine, fire, earthquake, and tidal wave; and now at the end I have become a victim myself. It is a good experience, even though I would not have chosen it.

Mud and water covered everything; basements were reservoirs of water, floors were ruined, foundations were undermined, and everything — bedding, clothing, rugs, and furniture — was soaking wet. As soon as it was possible to start the massive clean-up job, it was necessary to estimate the amount of the damage; and Tommy knew, as she watched the water being pumped from the basements, that all of the supplies which had been stored underground were a total loss. Their replacement alone would cost at least $5,000.

 So, along with a backache, there was a real heartache, for where was the money to come from? As the damage to the buildings was assessed, I estimated that the repairs and replacement costs would total nearly $20,000. However, we were not unmindful of our blessings, especially when we thought of the many villages which were wiped out completely; we were safe and had roofs over our heads. We were getting the hospital ready first, for disease was breaking out, and we had to be on the job.

Help came from the chapel at the nearby U. S. Air Base at Misawa, and, as Tommy's spirits rose, her sense of humor returned. "I told the Presbyterian chaplain who came that, if the Baptists didn't help me out, I would join the Presbyterians, and that would be a terrible blow to both denominations!"

The backache finally became just a memory as Kuji dried out and shoveled the mud from its shops and homes, and dikes were rebuilt and fields drained. The heartache was also alleviated and the worry lifted when the Baptist boards sent emergency financial help, and when the friends and churches who believed in Kuji rallied to raise money to repair the damaged buildings and replace the waterlogged supplies.

 It was a heart-warming experience to see the many, many friends the Kuji work had and the response they gave to our needs. It was like a beautiful rainbow after the flood.

However, this kind of help had become a part of the picture that was Kuji. So effective had been the ministry of Tommy and the Yahabas, and so dedicated had been their lives that there were always those who stood by to help in any emergency. Kuji was more than a place; it was people, and they had developed their own pattern for meeting community needs.

The day begins early at Kuji, for by five o'clock the cooks are lighting fires in the central kitchen and filling kettles with rice and soup for breakfast. At six o'clock fleeting figures cross the yard and climb the stairs of the Center building to gather in the library for a prayer meeting. Teachers from the schools, nurses from the hospital — all who wish to begin the day in prayer together meet for a few minutes of worship. Then the sound of a brisk march calls the staff members to the school yard for an exercise period, and by the time it is finished, the soup is steaming hot, and the rice is fluffy and warm. By seven-thirty there is a quiet hum of activity, and another day has begun; presently the school children fill the playground. The Kuji kindergarteners wear bright yellow caps and carry yellow shoulder bags marked with the school symbol, the beloved deer, Bambi. White-coated doctors start their rounds through the hospital wards, and, as they pass the dispensary, they nod to the mothers with babies on their backs and to the deeply-tanned men in the waiting room.

Tommy's day begins with private devotions, and then her daily schedule follows the routine of the Center as she joins fellow staff members for prayer meeting and for exercises. She plays the piano for the marching kindergarteners and teaches English conversation in the school. On Sundays she plays either the piano or the battered portable field organ for the worship service and for Sunday school. Often she is invited to speak at school or town meetings where her flair for communicating a mystic faith and a practical concern for daily living, well seasoned with humor, charms her audiences.

And what else does she do? Well, plenty! Often there are official visitors to entertain — men from the government offices, educational officials, or agriculturists. Visiting pastors sometimes come to speak in the church or go to the groups meeting farther out in the countryside. Wandering foreigners occasionally make their way to Kuji, and, when they do, city officials send a rush call for Tommy. When an American ship came into one of the small nearby ports, she not only interpreted for the visiting seamen, but she also arranged a baseball game with a local team.

In her kitchen is a small built-in breakfast table and bench, and this is her office from which she carries on an extensive correspondence and transacts necessary business. Her home is built western-style; but, since it lacks central heating, life in the winter revolves around the two stoves — one in the living room and one in the kitchen.

Active direction of the Center is Takeshi's responsibility, and, after sharing the early morning activities, he takes up his duties as director of the Center, pastor of the Church, and principal of the School. Often his day begins with a quick tour of the Center institutions. On the playground he holds a brief worship service for the children, and then, with all of the zest of a veteran soldier, he directs the marching drill which the children love. When the bell signals that they must enter their classes, he crosses to the hospital to check on the business activities, to inquire after the seriously ill patients, and to gather the staff together for a few minutes of rededication to the service of suffering humanity. Farm management is also a part of his day, and he may check on the seedlings which are being planted on the denuded hillsides or on the progress of experimental strip crops that grow in special test fields.

While there is much of the practical and administrative in Takeshi's daily round, there is also much of the spiritual and pastoral. He must find time for the preparation of sermons and other talks; he must find time for the pastoral care of his flock of baptized Christians; and he must find time for the troubled men and women who often seek his help.

And there must be ample time for business, for no business is conducted brusquely in Japan, and no visitor would think of stating the purpose of his visit until he had conformed to the proprieties. The Japanese have a word for this way of doing business — *sodan,* and it always includes the serving of tea and the casual conversation that eases social relationships. When Junko Yahaba was small, she was asked about her father's occupation, and, after a moment she replied, "He drinks tea for a living."

Kuni is principal of the kindergarten and head of the women's work of the Center. The Mothers' Club is her particular responsibility, and this group meets together for fellowship, for educational programs, and to plan projects for the benefit of the school and the community. Gentle, reserved, and yet a strong individual, Kuni bears out Tommy's original estimate of her: "Here is a girl who does not follow the herd." She occasionally resents the time-consuming character of doing business Japanese-style. "I sometimes ask myself at night, 'What have you done for the Lord's work today?' And I can only answer, 'Lord, I've served thirty cups of tea.'"

One of the postwar innovations of the Japanese judicial system is the family court. Kuni serves as counselor on the Kuji family court and is often called as an understanding adviser on domestic problems. She still cherishes the idea of the Christian home and the Christian family, even while recognizing that family life must often be sacrificed to the demands of the wider community.

Her daughter, Junko, remembers little of the hardships of her early years. Junko attended the Center school, and, while Tommy and Kuni rejoiced in her proficiency in English and in her talent for music, her father glowed with pride as she raced to victory in the annual athletic meets. After graduating from the Kuji Middle School, she entered Saint Margaret's High School for Girls in Tokyo, a Christian school established by the Episcopal Church. As a teenager she was troubled by the questions and doubts common to her generation in Japan, but she especially wanted to discover what it was that had kept her father and mother faithful in the hard, unrewarding years of work in Kuji:

> When I used to see how you had to struggle and suffer over Kuji all the time, and knew something of your problems and of your heartache, I felt that I wanted to get away and never return to work here; it was just too hard! But my heart has changed now, and I believe that God wants me in this hard place, and I plan to prepare for just that.

Kozo Yahaba is assistant pastor of the church and administrative director of the hospital, and, as such, his work is as demanding as that of his brother, Takeshi. He says:

> My work is now varied. My status is assistant minister, and that sounds awfully big when you have such a small church! However, I am not only assistant pastor, but assistant in tending to the chickens and in feeding the pigs, and in being business manager of the hospital. I am also assistant as head of the Sunday School and as director of the country work. I also drive the station wagon as an ambulance, and then I drive it as chauffeur for the doctors!

Kuni's two sisters, Kimi and Tsuyako, who joined her early in the Kuji venture, are graduates of Shokei and of the Tokyo Kindergarten Training School. They teach in the kindergarten and assist in all of the programs of religious education. When Kozo Yahaba settled down permanently in Kuji, he and Tsuyako were married. Now they have three sons, Maki, Kyo, and Kei, who do their best to keep life at the Center from being dull.

As the year for Tommy to retire drew near, she made arrangements to stay on in Kuji. Although she was past the age of sixty-five, her doctor assured her that she was strong enough to continue her work. Laying aside his stethoscope, he assured her, "You have a sixteen-year-old heart." In 1958, after forty-three

years in Japan, she found herself a much-honored senior missionary. As the moment of official retirement drew near, her
Japanese and American friends recognized her signal services and
sought to express their appreciation of her contributions to Christianity and to Japanese culture.

When the farm was dedicated, hundreds of friends came from
Iwate Ken, from Morioka and Sendai, and from Tokyo. They
came not only for the dedication, but to watch with pride the
awarding of the Imperial Decoration, *The Fifth Order of the
Sacred Jewel,* to Tommy. Kuni's uncle, Bishop Tomojiro Obara,
cut short a mission to South America to return and make the
main speech of the day, and amidst his tribute to the work that
Tommy had done in Kuji, he remembered the confusion she had
felt when she first heard the word *tamashii* and mistook it for
her own name. "*Tamashii* means soul," he said, "and to us *Tamashii,* or Thomasine, indeed means a great soul."

In June, 1959, Franklin College awarded her the honorary
degree of Doctor of Humane Letters, "as one whose entire career
beautifully symbolizes the motto of Franklin College, 'Christianity and Culture,' who has combined learning with compassion
in an area of great need, who has bridged the gulfs of race,
nation, language, and cultural heritage." When the doctoral hood
arrived from America, the Kuji Mothers' Club held a reception
in her honor.

 It was a family affair; only those connected with the Center
were invited, and it was held out of doors. The kindergarten
performed nobly, each class by itself and then all of them together, and the Shogakko (Elementary school) and the Chugakko (Middle school) sang beautifully. There were speeches,
and flowers were presented by the smallest children. Afterwards
they set up tables with all sorts of Japanese food, and we all
had lunch together and a social time, and then they sang some
more songs. It was all quite lovely, and the Mothers' Club took
the whole responsibility.

In 1960, the Honorable Frank S. Records, Mayor of Franklin,
Indiana, and the Honorable Gyobun Yamauchi, Mayor of Kuji,
Japan, issued proclamations declaring the two communities to be
sister cities. The Mayor of Kuji wrote this letter to the Mayor
of Franklin:

From your city in 1915 came a young lady to work with us. She has had honors bestowed on her from your side of the Pacific and from our side . . . in Japan as well as in America. Because we respect and honor Miss Allen and want her to spend her life here, we as a City Council in October, 1959, voted unanimously to make her an honorary citizen of Kuji. . . . Miss Allen has been a real bridge across the dividing ocean and it is an honor for us to have her in our midst.

Appropriately formal exchanges sealed the declaration, and in Kuji a grand ceremony was held in the Chamber of the City Assembly. Seventy officials gathered under crossed American and Japanese flags to accept the proclamation and to listen to Tommy's response. She asked for understanding of the real purpose of the Center and of the goals of spiritual training to which the Center was dedicated.

As she spoke, Tommy recalled that the Japanese Protestant Church had celebrated its centennial year in 1959. The Church then numbered about 350,000 members, and it was noted for the intellectual quality of its Christianity. Protestant Japanese professed a biblical and orthodox Christianity which emphasized doctrinal authority and exemplary moral behavior. Emphases on social action and liturgical beauty were somewhat lacking, perhaps due to the small number of Christians and the relative youth of the church. Tommy had gone to Tokyo for the Centennial.

 It was truly inspiring to see at least 10,000 Christians in one worship service; imagine that in Japan! Nearly all of the church congregations are so small that it helped all of us to be in a really big meeting. Like Jacob, I guess we all needed to see the wagons at times. Representatives from all over the world brought or sent greetings, and that made it worldwide in scope.

It is hard to equate all of that with Kuji, for Tokyo and its churches belong to the twentieth century, and here in Kuji we are back where the first missionaries were in the nineteenth century. It is discouraging, but it is necessary, and maybe in another hundred years some results will be seen here, too. Do you remember the story of the man who had tried so hard to win people and was so discouraged at the small number? He talked it over with Jesus and came away smiling. When his friends asked him what made him so happy, he answered, "Why Jesus said, 'Four is a very large number indeed.'" *Kuji has always had a large number!*

Chapter Nineteen

ONE HUNDRED YEARS IS BUT A DAY

> Over the western sea, hither from Niphon come,
> Courteous, the swart-cheek'd two-sworded envoys,
> Leaning back in their open barouches, bare-headed, impassive,
> Ride to-day through Manhattan. . . .
> For not the envoys, not the tann'd Japanee from his island only;
> Lithe and silent, the Hindoo appears — the Asiatic continent itself appears — the Past, the dead,
> The murky night-morning of wonder and fable, inscrutable,
> The envelop'd mysteries, the old and unknown hive-bees,
> The North — the sweltering South — eastern Assyria — the Hebrews — the Ancient of Ancients,
> Vast desolated cities — the gliding Present — all of these, and more, are in the pagent-procession.
> Comrade Americanos! — to us, then, at last, the Orient comes. [11]

EXUBERANT WALT WHITMAN poured out his feeling when, in 1860, the first Japanese Embassy visited the United States. With characteristic understatement, Second Ambassador Norimasa Muragaki expressed his feeings about the mission.

> From now, the bright moonlight of our country
> Will be admired by the peoples of the strange lands.

One hundred years later the two nations observed the centennial anniversary of the visit of Ambassador Muragaki and his colleagues with assurances of friendship, visits of good will, and volcanic outbursts of violence. During the preceding century the

---

[11] Walt Whitman, "A Broadway Pageant," *Leaves of Grass.*

Orient had come to the comrade Americans, and its bright moonlight had also been admired by the peoples of the strange lands. Through the century marked by both cooperative friendship and bitter conflict, men of integrity from both countries had sought to bridge the gap of understanding that plagued the relations of the two countries. Many of them echoed the lines which Second Ambassador Muragaki penned on his first night in America.

> In the same sky over the strange land
> Glows even the same spring moon, misty-veiled.

Although rioting Japanese students forced the Japanese government to cancel an invitation previously extended to President Dwight D. Eisenhower to visit Japan in the Centennial spring of 1960, they could not destroy the lasting bonds that had been forged between the two nations by dedicated men and women. Nor could they undermine the bridge that had been built through service and sacrifice, education and appreciation, and fellowship and friendship.

The Japanese selected a "List of Contributors" to be honored at this time by the Association for the Japan — United States Amity and Trade Centennial. Those contributors included Americans who had made outstanding contributions in four different areas: religious and educational; economic and industrial; political and diplomatic; and social and cultural. Chosen for her social and cultural achievements, Tommy was invited to Tokyo for the celebration.

 The program was very lovely and dignified; we each had to go up and receive our citation, and there were several speeches and congratulatory messages by Mr. Kosaka, the minister of Foreign Affairs and our Ambassador. We were also given a large Urushi etching (a special type of lacquer print produced on paper or silk) of the Japanese vessel, the *Kanrin Maru*, which took the first Japanese delegation to America in 1860. Then they had a truly remarkable film, *The Bridge That Spans the Pacific*, which showed the history of Japanese-American relations. Woodcuts were used to show life in feudal Japan, while photographs and newsreel clips were used for the later years. It was especially well done!

In one part of the hall, pictures of many of the 298 people being honored were on display. There were pictures of many who had died or were retired in America, and it was good to "see" some of my old friends in that way. There were seven Baptists on the list, and I am the only one still in Japan.

The list included many interesting and colorful people: There were the early Americans, the first to reach Japan, the adventurous disciples of the doctrine of Manifest Destiny who carried the American flag across the Pacific. Important among them was Matthew Calbraith Perry, whose name has passed into the annals of history as the man who opened Japan. Then followed a listing of missionaries and theologians, scholars and educators, politicians and diplomats, agriculturalists and technicians, and social and cultural leaders, each of whom had made a special contribution to the life of Japan. Although Tommy enjoyed being among those so honored, it was just as exciting to find the name of her one-time co-worker, William Axling, and her friends, Mr. and Mrs. Donald J. Mac Kenzie. Mr. and Mrs. Mac Kenzie pioneered in developing the tea packing industry in the Shizuoka area, laying the foundations for a profitable export business for Japan. Mr. Mac Kenzie had assembled a notable collection of far eastern art, while Mrs. Mac Kenzie's generous philanthropy and hospitality became legendary. For Tommy the Mac Kenzie home was a haven of occasional relaxation from the rigors of Kuji.

Together Tommy and Mrs. Mac Kenzie read the names on the list and looked at the pictures, seeing again the faces of beloved friends, both the living and the dead. Then the reception was over, and it was time for Tommy to catch the train at Ueno Station and return to Kuji. She plunged through the swarming station jammed with hustling travelers and boarded the train that would carry her north through Sendai and Morioka and finally to Shiriuchi and the branch line to Kuji. It was nearly midnight when she had time to settle in her seat, relax, and think.

 Again I was reminded of the past: The long, cold treks over mountain, hill, and plain on relief trips during famine, earthquake, and tidal wave; the starting of day nurseries and kindergartens; and the beginning of medical and educational work for country folk whose lives are so drab. I was the "victim" of all these honors, but the real thanks and homage belong to Mr. and Mrs. Yahaba who, by their consecrated and dedicated lives, have made the Kuji work possible, and to all those who, by their prayers and gifts, have pulled me through the valleys and

up the mountains. Perhaps I have learned through them a bit
more about the necessity of lifting my eyes to the mountains
when walking in the valley and keeping my faith that there is
always a *high road*.

Forty-five years had passed since the young girl from Indiana
had landed in Yokohama. Propelled by the zeal of her mother
and the example of her sister, and filled with the idealism of the
Student Volunteers, she was ready to do her share in winning
the world for Christ "in one generation." She thought she could
do her share by following the path that seemed to lie straight
ahead, leading her to the cloistered atmosphere of a mission
school for girls. Her share, she had thought, was teaching Bible
and English classes and holding meetings for women and for
children. "I played all of the accompaniments," she wrote in her
diary in 1915, "and believed that this was my proper role; not
leadership, not pioneering, not controversy." But Kuji with its
tragic poverty and its tenacious traditionalism was then a world
she could hardly imagine.

Forty-five years had passed, and Thomasine Allen was now a
senior missionary, retired from active service as a representative
of the society; but she had not retired from Kuji. She was needed
in the school and the kindergarten; she was needed in the church;
and she was needed to help to carry the financial load. "I *must*
live to get this place self-supporting — or anyway, so *I* think!"
But she had no illusions now about what "this generation" could
accomplish; instead she had an abiding faith in what God could
do and had done.

It was morning now, and the train pulled into the Morioka
station. Vendors came to the train hawking ice cream bars and
box lunches and pots of steaming hot tea. Memories of her first
independent venture, the Shinjo Center in Morioka, flooded in.

 It seems to me, as I look over the years, that God's message
to me was, "I want to work through you in that isolated, difficult place, and I will show you the way to soften the soil. It
must be by *blood, sweat, and tears;* the blood of sacrifice, the
sweat of physical and spiritual labor, and the tears of heartbreak, discouragement, and disappointment." Then I thought
of St. Theresa when she prayed, "God, if you treat all of our
friends as you do me, it is no wonder that you have so few."

At the junction town of Shiriuchi, Tommy left the Aomori Express and climbed the familiar steps to cross the tracks. As she entered the bare waiting room, the station master came to bow his greetings and invited her to wait in his office for the next train. Gratefully she accepted and followed him into a room with comfortable chairs and a little electric heater to take the chill from the air. After tea and a bowl of noodles at noon, she boarded the train for the last leg of the long journey. Then the country people piled aboard with all their bags and bundles and the train started its journey up the coast to Kuji. Tommy again had time for retrospection:

 As we bumped along the tracks, the drabness of everything impressed me anew, and I wondered how long it would be before the Light would shine, transforming lives and their surroundings. The autumn foliage which had given so much beauty and color to the scene was gone, and the snow which conceals so much of the ugliness and covers everything with a mantle of purity had not yet come; so there was nothing to relieve the drabness of the dirty, shoddy little shacks called homes. This drabness of people and scenery was depressing, and I wondered what possible joy the people who live and work in such conditions could have from life. Then, as the train climbed to higher levels, the distant scene, the beautiful mountains, and the vast expanse of sky reminded me that we must take the long view and never be too discouraged at the slow pace of change. In time, the drabness of home and life will be changed to color, light, and joy as we with God endeavor to be creators of a better tomorrow.

This was Tommy's treasure to share — the way to a better tomorrow.

Appendix:

SOME HELP WITH JAPANESE WORDS

THE PRONUNCIATION OF JAPANESE is a fairly simple matter. Consonants almost always have the same pronunciation as in English, except that the *g* is always hard. Vowels do not vary in their sound; *a* is sounded like the *a* in *father*, *o* like the *o* in *hoe*, *e* like the *e* in *net*, *i* like the *ee* in *week*, and *u* like the *u* in *sue*. Each vowel is sounded, the most common double vowels being *ai* like the *ai* in *aisle*, *ei* like the *ei* in *vein*, and *au* like the *ow* in *cow*. Doubled consonants are sounded individually; with a little practice one can learn to sound the two *k*'s in such a word as *Hokkaido*.

Japanese names are given in accord with English language usage, first names first, and family names last.

GLOSSARY

aisu kurimu — ice cream.

akabo — a redcap.

Amaterasu-omikami — the legendary sun goddess and ancestress of the emperors of Japan.

Bodhisattvas — in Buddhism, supernatural beings qualified for entry into Paradise but sharing their merit with human supplicants.

Buddhism — the faith professed by the majority of the Japanese. Founded by the Indian prince, Gautama Buddha in the preChristian era, it became prominent in China and moved into Japan in the sixth century.

158

Buddhas — images of Gautama Buddha.

Bushido — the way or code of the warrior, stressing manly dignity, self sacrifice, and loyalty.

Chugakko — middle or junior high school.

Daikyo — the Great Religion, a simple creed of the Meiji Era, 1868-1912, not widely accepted.

Fukuin Maru — the Gospel Ship, captained by Philip Bickel, which sailed the Japan Inland Sea for many years. After World War II a new vessel took its place.

hakama — a pleated, divided skirt worn over kimono in traditional Japanese formal dress.

Izanagi and *Izanami* — legendary creators of Japanese islands.

Jimmu Tenno — first emperor of Japan.

Jizo-San — a patron god in the Buddhist faith who looks after little children.

kamishibai — literally, the paper theater, in which stories are illustrated by large, colorful pictures.

kawase — a postal money order.

kimono — a long robe held with an elaborate girle, called an *obi*.

Kojiki — history book written about A.D. 712.

kotatsu — an opening in the floor of a Japanese room which contains a firepot, and is often covered by a table and a quilt to preserve the heat.

koto — a stringed musical instrument.

Kotogakko — high school.

Kwannon — a goddess of mercy and benevolence in oriental religions.

matsu — the Japanese pine tree, symbolizing courage in the face of adversity.

mukashi-mukashi — once upon a time.

moxa — a medical treatment which involves the burning of bits of powdered wood on certain areas of the patient's body.

Nara — an early capital of Japan.

neko — a cat.

Nihon Shoki — the great official history of Japan, written in A.D. 720 and based on the earlier *Kojiki*.

sakura — the famous flowering cherry trees of Japan, which bloom in early spring for one or two weeks and symbolize the willingness of the *samurai* to die in battle at the height of his manhood.

samisen — a three-stringed banjo-like musical instrument.

samurai — a Japanese warrior.

Sensei — teacher (a title indicating a position of great prestige).

Shinto — the national faith of Japan.

Shogakko — elementary school.

shogun — a military ruler of Japan who governed in the name of the Emperor.

Shushin — moral training.

soba — thin buckwheat noodles served in a spiced broth, often seasoned with chopped onion and red pepper.

sodan — a conference or consultation.

Soga — one of the court families in Kyoto, selected to test the newly-imported faith of Buddhism in the sixth century.

sukiyaki — a popular Japanese dish, thin slices of beef cooked with slivers of vegetables and seasoned with soy sauce.

tamashii — the soul.

Tanabata — a Japanese festival celebrated in midsummer.

tatami — rice-straw mats, used to floor Japanese rooms. Woven around a wooden frame, *tatami* mats are of standard dimensions, six feet long and three feet wide. The size of a room is often described as a six-mat or an eight-mat room.

Tendai — form of Buddhism introduced into Japan from China in the ninth century, which helped to make it possible for Buddhism and Shinto to develop side by side in Japan.

Tokugawa Period — from 1600 to 1867, when the Tokugawa clan controlled the shogunate; the period of Japan's seclusion from contact with the outside world.

torii — a gateway at the entrance to a Shinto shrine, consisting of two uprights supporting a curved lintel with a straight crosspiece below.

ume — Japanese flowering plum which blooms in the late winter or early spring, symbolizing purity of heart and forbearance in hardship.

Urushi etching — painting with lacquer on paper or silk.

yochien — kindergarten.